Heroes of Bomber Command

CAMBRIDGESHIRE

GRAHAM SMITH

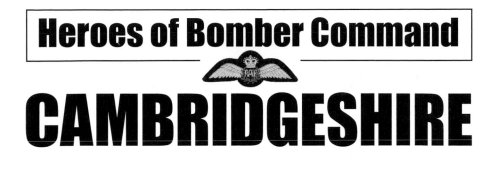

COUNTRYSIDE BOOKS
NEWBURY BERKSHIRE

First published 2007
© Graham Smith 2007

All rights reserved. No reproduction permitted without
the prior permission of the publisher:

COUNTRYSIDE BOOKS
3 Catherine Road,
Newbury, Berkshire.

To view our complete range of books,
please visit us at
www.countrysidebooks.co.uk

ISBN 978 1 84674 039 8

The cover picture shows a Mosquito of No 128 Squadron
at Wyton about to leave on the 'Berlin Express'

Designed by Peter Davies, Nautilus Design
Produced through MRM Associates Ltd, Reading
Printed by Cambridge University Press

CONTENTS

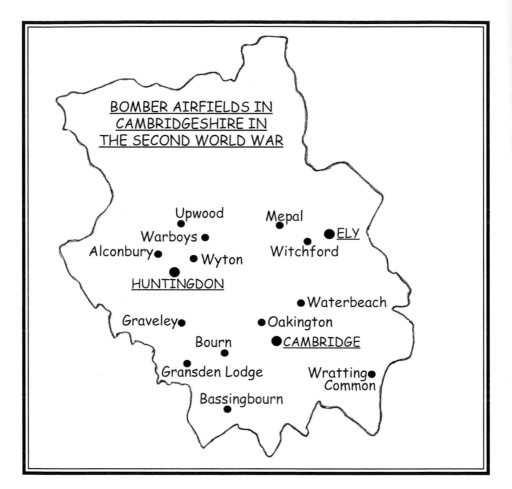

BOMBER AIRFIELDS IN
CAMBRIDGESHIRE IN
THE SECOND WORLD WAR

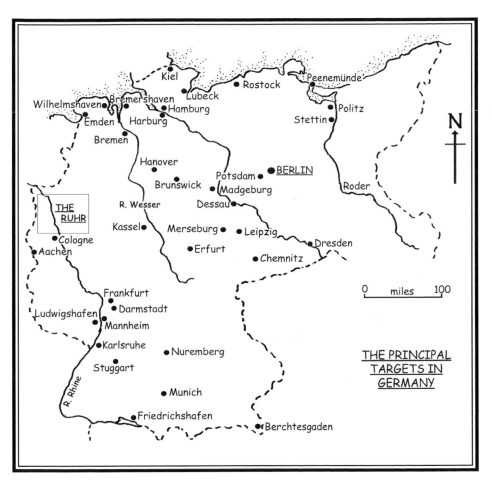

See page 100 for the map of the Ruhr.

Introduction

Sir Arthur Harris, Bomber Command's most celebrated Commander-in-Chief, stated in his book *Bomber Offensive* that approximately 125,000 aircrew served in Bomber Command during the Second World War; no less than 55,500 of these airmen were killed, some 8,400 wounded and over 9,830 made prisoners of war. This was an enormous human sacrifice to pay for the strategic bombing offensive; the Command's fatalities were over three-quarters of the R.A.F.'s total loss of aircrew for the whole of the war.

The bomber crews were engaged in a special type of warfare; a matter of hours separated them from the relative peace and tranquillity of the English countryside and a flight into hell. They had to contend with adverse weather, intense cold, physical and mental fatigue, phalanxes of searchlights, heavy and intense flak and the *Luftwaffe*'s night fighters, before returning, if they were lucky, across a hostile North Sea often in damaged aircraft before landing safely; a blessed return to some form of normality but with the sure and certain knowledge that the next night they would face such horrors again, and again and again until their tours were completed or their luck deserted them and they did not return, like so many of their friends and colleagues. Despite this they did not receive any special Campaign medal.

For many years the 'Fighter Boys' of the Battle of Britain have quite rightly received endless acclaim, with countless books published on their part in the famous Battle. Until recently, scant regard or honour had been accorded to all the brave and sterling efforts of the 'Bomber Men', although a number of publications have lately somewhat righted the balance.

It is quite impossible to find adequate words to describe the immense contribution made by the men of Bomber Command. Even Sir Arthur Harris found it a difficult task: 'There are no words with which I can do justice to the aircrew who fought under my command. There is no parallel in warfare to such courage and determination ... it was the courage of the small hours with long drawn out apprehensions of "going over the top". They were without exception volunteers, for no man was trained for air-crew with the R.A.F. who did not volunteer for this. Such devotion must not be forgotten. It is unforgettable by anyone whose contacts gave them knowledge and understanding of what these young men experienced and faced...'.

During almost six years of war waged by the crews of Bomber Command many heroes emerged and twenty-one Victoria Crosses were awarded to

Bomber Command airmen; most of their names are still remembered and celebrated over sixty years later. However, every single airman who flew with Bomber Command deserves to be considered a hero; whether in fact they completed just a single mission or indeed many, many more. It is to all those brave young airmen – their average age was twenty-two years – that I very humbly dedicate this book; and more especially to my friends of No 156, one of the four original Pathfinder squadrons. As their squadron motto proclaims – 'We Light the Way'.

Graham Smith

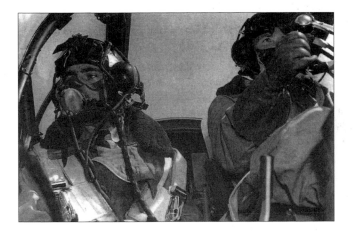

Acknowledgments

I am deeply indebted to a number of people for their assistance during the preparation of this book: Mrs Myra Wilkes, Charlie Chapman and David Chamberlin were especially generous with their help. A number of other individuals gave freely of their time to provide a number of photographs.

Chapter 1

'Strike Hard, Strike Sure'

During the 1920s and 1930s the Royal Air Force's role in a future war had never been in any doubt, the predominant concept was that of a powerful heavy bomber force striking into the heart of the enemy's territory. Sir Hugh Trenchard, Marshal of the Royal Air Force, was the leading proponent of this doctrine: he was utterly convinced that the main, if not the only, *raison d'etre* of the Service lay in the use of heavy bombers; he was once described as 'the patron saint of modern air power'. The origins of this tenet can be traced back to the latter years of the First World War, partly as a result of the German raids on London with Gotha and Giant bombers and the formation of the Independent Air Force in June 1918 – 'to carry the war into Germany by attacking her industry, commerce and population'; this Force was commanded by Trenchard.

In 1928 Trenchard stated: 'It is air power that can pass over the enemy navies and armies and penetrate the air defences and attack the centres of production, transportation and communication from which the enemy's war effort is maintained ... and it will be in this manner that air superiority will be maintained and not by the direct destruction of armed forces'. Allied to this unwavering conviction was his dismissive view of the role of fighters in an air war, which he considered would never be a match for a strong force of heavy bombers; therefore fighters were relegated to a minor role in the pre-war Royal Air Force.

The cult of the omnipotent bomber was further emphasised in November 1932 when Stanley Baldwin, the Conservative leader, famously declared that 'there is no power on earth that can protect him [the man in the street] from being bombed. Whatever people may tell him, the bomber will always get through'. This deeply engrained philosophy ensured that bomber squadrons outnumbered fighter squadrons by two to one and bomber pilots became the 'elite' of the R.A.F., almost a privileged class. It was not until the Battle of Britain that 'The Few' stole the thunder from their colleagues in Bomber Command.

In 1934 the first of eight R.A.F. Expansion Schemes was introduced, which ensured that within five years the Service had almost trebled in size and strength. This remarkable growth also brought in its wake a radical and major reorganisation. In 1936 the 'Air Defence of Great Britain', which had controlled both bomber and fighter squadrons, was replaced by four separate and functional Commands – Bomber, Coastal, Fighter and Training – each with a precise and specific role and divided into a number of Groups. Under the new system the individual Air Officers Commanding were responsible for the planning and development of their Commands, with the Chief of the Air Staff remaining in overall control of operational policy.

Bomber Command was formed at Uxbridge on 14th July 1936 under the control of Air Marshal Sir John Steel and comprised three Groups, which had increased to six by the outbreak of war in 1939, numbering fifty-three squadrons; although twenty were engaged in training and considered non-operational with another ten despatched to France as the Advanced Air Striking Force. Thus Bomber Command had just twenty-three operational squadrons – barely two hundred and eighty aircraft – operating from a mere twenty-seven airfields. By March 1945 Bomber Command was at the zenith of its power, a massive force of over 2,200 aircraft in ninety-seven squadrons – a highly technical and totally professional strike force of terrifying and awesome power. Eighteen squadrons were based at eleven bomber stations in Cambridgeshire, most of them serving in 8 Group – the legendary Pathfinder Force.

Although R.A.F. squadron and station badges were first introduced in 1936, Bomber Command's badge was not formally approved by H.M. King George VI until March 1947; the thunderbolt depicted on the badge represented the Command's striking force and the Astral Crown showed its success. The Command took as its motto '*Strike Hard Strike Sure*'. For the next twenty-one years Bomber Command remained the largest force in

Bomber Command's badge was formally approved in March 1947.

the R.A.F. until it merged with Fighter Command on 1st May 1968 to form Strike Command, as it is still known today.

The rapid expansion of the R.A.F. necessitated the provision of many new airfields for the additional planned squadrons. In 1933 there were only twenty-seven airfields housing operational squadrons. The new stations, many of which would house bomber squadrons, were required to be located in the eastern counties, those nearest to the perceived enemy – Germany. Previously the relatively few bomber stations had been sited in southern and central England.

During the First World War a number of landing grounds in Cambridgeshire had been used, mainly for flying training, therefore it was no surprise that the Air Ministry sought suitable sites in the county for its new bomber stations. Ultimately five sites were selected, although only three new 'Expansion' stations, as they were then known, opened before the outbreak of war. It should be noted that some of these, and the later wartime stations, were not then in Cambridgeshire, but for the purposes of this account all that were, or are now, sited within the county boundaries have been included.

The first Expansion station was located at Wyton, three miles north-east of Huntingdon; it formally opened in July 1936 and was originally allocated to 3 Group, which had formed on 1st May 1936 at Andover. Over seventy years later it is still an active R.A.F. station. The first bomber squadron to occupy the new station was No 139, which reformed there on 3rd September, followed on 12th December by another reformed squadron – No 114. Both could proudly trace their origins back to the First World War, and both were equipped with Hawker Hinds, the last biplane light bomber. With its open cockpit it looked as if it belonged to a different age of flying, although the Hind had first flown only two years earlier. It was an improved version of the remarkable Hart and was really an interim replacement for the Hart and moreover a stop-gap until the new planned monoplanes began to enter the Service.

Hinds entered the Service in late 1935; they had a top speed of 186 mph, carried up to 500 lbs of bombs with a range of some 450 miles and were armed with two machine guns. They were liked by their crews, who claimed that they were 'a delight to fly'. By early 1937 there were over four hundred and fifty in service ultimately equipping forty squadrons; nevertheless just

11

Hawker Hinds of No XV Squadron; the last biplane light bombers.

two years later they had virtually disappeared from front-line squadrons. No 139 Squadron also had a number of Hawker Audaxes, another Hart variant, which had been specially developed for Army Co-operation duties. They had first entered the Service in 1932 and over seven hundred were produced; they were equipped with a hook to pick up messages and also stores containers under the wings. In the Service they were jokingly referred to as 'Arts with 'ooks!

Wyton deserves a special place in the history of the R.A.F. as it was the first to receive the legendary Bristol Blenheim, which spearheaded Bomber Command's daylight operations in the early war years. The Bristol 142, as it was originally designated, made its maiden flight in April 1935 and had been designed and built at the

The cockpit of a Blenheim I.
(via J. Adams)

12

behest of Lord Rothermere, the proprietor of the *Daily Mail*; he named it *Britain First* and, after the Air Ministry had requested that they might retain it for a period of testing to evaluate its potential as a light bomber, he generously donated it to the nation. The Bristol Aeroplane Company had already designed an improved military version, a twin-engine medium day bomber – 142M; it was of all-metal construction and was capable of carrying a 1,000 lb bomb load over a range of 1,125 miles with a top speed of 279 mph, which was then far faster than any R.A.F. fighter. It required a three-man crew and was armed with a .303 inch machine-gun in the port wing and a Vickers 'K' gun in the dorsal turret. The Air Ministry was so impressed that one hundred and fifty were immediately ordered 'off the drawing board', a rare occurrence in those days. The following year over five hundred and seventy were ordered. The Air Ministry obviously felt that it had 'a winner' on its hands.

In May 1936 it was officially named the Blenheim Mark I and two months later (25th June) the prototype made its first flight. The first Blenheim was delivered to 114 Squadron at Wyton on 1st March 1937 and when the squadron displayed their new aircraft at the R.A.F. Hendon display in the

Blenheim I (K7037) joined 114 Squadron at Wyton on 17th March 1937.

summer, it created immense interest and great excitement with its high speed and modern appearance and was soon dubbed 'the Wonder Bomber'. In July, 139 Squadron began to convert to Blenheims and by the end of the year another three squadrons had been similarly equipped.

In early January 1937 the second Expansion station opened in Cambridgeshire, situated in the parish of Upwood, less than two miles south-west of Ramsey. Like all these new stations the airfield was grass-covered and was allocated to 2 Group, which had been the Command's first Group to form at Abingdon on 20th March 1936; it was different from the other two Groups in that it was always intended to act as an army support force. In 1938 the Group's headquarters moved to Wyton.

Upwood's first squadron, No 52, arrived in March with Hinds, followed a few days later by No 63, also equipped with Hinds as well as a number of Audaxes. However, within two months, No 63 became the first squadron to receive the latest light bomber – the Fairey Battle; a sleek single-engine low-wing monoplane that had first flown on 10th March 1936. It had a maximum speed of 240 mph and a 1,000 lb bomb load; however, it was only lightly armed with one .303 inch Browning machine gun in the port wing and a single Vickers gun aft. In September 1939 ten Battle squadrons formed the Advanced Air Striking Force but, in May 1940, its inferior performance and fire-power were harshly exposed by the *Luftwaffe* in the French skies.

In 1937 the R.A.F. was still a small and select, but highly professional, Service and numbered a mere 68,000 men. Most of its senior officers had flown operationally during the First World War; the majority of its pilots had been recruited from the public schools and had graduated from the Service's own college at Cranwell. They were predominantly regular officers but a fair number had entered via the short-service commission entry, which had been introduced in 1932. Many of the ground crews and sergeant pilots had served

Fairey Battle of No 52 Squadron at Upwood.

Air Chief Marshal Sir Hugh Trenchard inspects the first aircraft apprentices to pass out of Halton, 17th December 1924.

their apprenticeship at the Apprentices School at Halton. Both inculcated a rigorous standard of discipline perhaps more suited to the regular Army rather than the unique demands that would soon be placed on pilots and crews. It was this hard core of officers and airmen that formed the backbone of the Service in the early war years.

This somewhat elitist Service was supported by a number of squadrons of the Auxiliary Air Force, the enthusiastic 'weekend pilots'. Without question, whether regulars, short-service or reservists, all were utterly devoted to the Service. This dedication and fervour remained steadfast throughout the war, despite the intolerable and harrowing demands placed upon the aircrews and ground personnel. The most fundamental change as far as the Service was concerned, was the introduction, in 1936, of the Volunteer Reserve as a reserve for the regular Air Force. It was designed to attract 'young men of our cities, without any class distinctions ... to open the new force to the whole middle class in the widest sense of that term, namely the complete range of the output of public, grammar and secondary schools'. It offered opportunities to young men who never visualized that they would be selected for flying training with the regular Royal Air Force. The V.R. was expected to produce eight hundred pilots each year, but the scheme was far more successful than the wildest hopes. On 1st September 1939 the R.A.F.V.R.'s aircrew strength was over 10,200, of which some 6,400 were pilots, mostly sergeants.

Air Chief Marshal Sir Edgar R. Ludlow-Hewitt, D.S.O., M.C., Legion of Honour, was appointed the Air Officer Commander-in-Chief of Bomber Command on 12th September 1937. He had qualified as a pilot back in August 1914 and had seen active service in France. It fell to him to prepare Bomber Command for the impending war. It was a formidable task, which he recognised in November when he reported: '[It] is entirely unprepared for war, unable to operate except in fair weather and is extremely vulnerable both in the air and on the ground'. 'Ludlow', as he was known, guided the Command through its re-equipment and rapid pre-war expansion, and despite its failings and shortcomings, the Command owed him a deep debt of gratitude, if only for his courageous decision in January 1939 to establish

Air Chief Marshal Sir Edgar Ludlow-Hewitt was A.O.C.-in-C., Bomber Command from September 1937 to April 1940. (R.A.F. Museum)

a proper training and conversion regime with the formation of 'Reserve' or 'Pool' squadrons.

In March 1938 the last of the county's pre-war airfields opened at Bassingbourn, about four miles north of Royston directly to the west of the A14 main road. Before it was officially opened two Hind squadrons arrived – 104 and 108 – and the station was placed in 2 Group, as there was now a positive attempt by the Air Ministry to concentrate a Group's squadrons in the same area. During the summer both squadrons were equipped with Blenheims as more emerged from the production lines.

During the spring of 1938 the Air Ministry acquired some one hundred and fifty acres of land to the east of Alconbury Hill, with plans to develop it into a satellite landing ground. It had been considering the dispersal of operational aircraft in the event of air raids and such satellite airfields were thought to offer the solution. They had to be within reasonable distance of the parent station with good communications. If necessary, operations could be mounted from these basic landing grounds, but it would require the necessary fuel, ammunition and bombs to be transported by road. Thus Alconbury became the first planned satellite airfield and, as such, the theory was first tested in May 1938 when No 63's Battles used the landing ground. Only the most basic facilities were provided, the crews were accommodated under canvas and the aircraft returned to Upwood for fuelling, maintenance and repair.

Despite this apparently professional Service there were some glaring defects in the operational training of pilots and crews, more particularly in Bomber Command. It had long been the responsibility of squadrons to train their newly qualified pilots and observers in operational techniques. Navigation hardly merited a mention but map reading did; 'air navigation' became the art of following railway lines, known as 'Bradshawing' from the famous railway timetables. During 1936/7 well over four hundred forced landings had been made as a result of crews not knowing their position. Night flying received scant prominence; in 1937 only eighty-four of the Command's pilots were qualified for night flying, which is perhaps not too surprising considering that in the following year less than 10% of its flying hours were conducted at night. Obviously the airmen's old adage 'Only owls and fools fly by night' died hard. Sir Edgar Ludlow-Hewitt maintained that 40% of his crews were unable to find a target in a friendly city in broad daylight, let alone at night!

The concept of a dedicated bomber crew had not yet been realised. Wireless operators and air gunners were skilled tradesmen who had volunteered for flying duties on a part-time basis, mainly for the extra flying pay. They received little training for their duties on board. Aerial gunnery was notoriously weak in the pre-war Royal Air Force. Indeed it was not until December 1939 that air gunners were made full-time crew members and given the rank of sergeant along with their half-wing 'AG'.

The problems of operational training were somewhat resolved by the allocation, in January 1939, of fifteen of the precious front-line squadrons to undertake the necessary conversion and operational training of new pilots and crew within each Group. They became known as Group Pool Squadrons and on 2nd September they were transferred into a new Group – No 6 (Training). The establishment of these squadrons impinged heavily on the three bomber stations in Cambridgeshire. On 17th March the two squadrons at Upwood, 52 and 63, were designated training units, followed in May by 104 and 108 Squadrons at Bassingbourn. This left Wyton as the only operational station in the county and during 1939 the crews received the aircraft in which they would go to war.

After the success of the Blenheim Mark I, the Air Ministry considered that it could be developed into a general reconnaissance aircraft for Coastal Command. The Bristol Aeroplane Company produced Type 149, which was based on the Mark I but provided with additional fuel tanks and more powerful Bristol Mercury XV engines. However, the most striking difference was a lengthened nose, an extra 3 ft, which provided a position for the observer/radio operator ahead of and to the right of the pilot. When the prototype first flew on 24th September 1937 it was called *Bolinbroke* but this name was dropped for the Mark IV when the aircraft was developed for Bomber Command. The IVs, or 'long nosed' Blenheims, had an increased range of 1,460 miles and a slightly lower maximum speed of 266 mph. Besides the normal bomb load of 1,000 lbs, external racks were fitted to carry an additional 320 lbs of bombs and also its armament had been strengthened by the addition of one .303 gun beneath the nose.

The first Blenheim IVs were delivered to 90 Squadron on 22nd March 1939. The Air Ministry had decided that the Group would be totally

Blenheim IVs of No 139 Squadron.

equipped with Blenheims, and Wyton's first Mark IVs arrived on 27th April for 114 Squadron, followed by 139's on 13th July. At the outbreak of war the R.A.F. had over 1,000 Blenheims on strength, more than any other type of aircraft, although only 190 were Mark IVs. On 2nd September 1939, No 2 Group had seven Blenheim IV squadrons including the two based at Wyton, which operated as No 82 Wing.

Despite all the precious resources devoted to Bomber Command during the immediate pre-war years, the Command was ill-prepared for the task ahead. Although its crews were highly trained in actual flying they had scant experience of long-range flying, particularly at night, and furthermore of precise navigation. Few crews had flown with a full bomb load even by day. Their equipment was barely adequate; fuel tanks and systems were unprotected, as indeed were the pilots, from bullet and shell damage, heating was sadly lacking for high-altitude flying, radio, bombing and navigational systems were unsatisfactory and the defensive armament against enemy fighters was woefully inadequate. The *Official History of the Strategic Air Offensive* commented:

> **When war came in 1939 Bomber Command was not trained or equipped either to penetrate into enemy territory by day or to find its target areas, let alone its targets by night...[It] was above all an investment in the future.**

Thus Bomber Command entered its six long years of battle. The die was cast, the crews waited for the anticipated War Telegram and then their ordeal would begin.

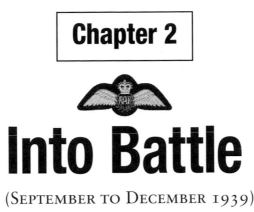

Chapter 2

Into Battle

(September to December 1939)

At three minutes past noon on 3rd September 1939, a Blenheim IV (N6215) of 139 Squadron left Wyton on the R.A.F.'s first operational sortie of the war, another notable first for this famous bomber station. Actually at this time 139 was the only operational squadron based in Cambridgeshire; the previous day No 114 had moved to Hullavington under the Air Ministry's 'Scatter Plans' when it had been decreed that several bomber squadrons should be dispersed away from their operational stations in the event of war, a precautionary and temporary measure in case of a pre-emptive enemy strike on airfields in East Anglia.

Flying Officer Andrew McPherson and his crew – Commander

Record of the first operational sortie of the war – Wyton, 3rd September 1939.
(The National Archives)

(*2608–226) Wl. 28300–1377 54.000 11/38 T.S. 667					Appendix ...	R.A.F. Form 541.
OPERATIONS RECORD BOOK.						
DETAIL OF WORK CARRIED OUT.						
From 1201 hrs. 3 / 9 / 39 to 2359 hrs. 8 / 9 / 39 By 139 Sqdn.					No. of pages used for day ... 1 ...	
Aircraft Type and No.	Crew.	Duty.	Time Up.	Time Down.	Remarks.	References.
Blenheim MK. IV. N6215.	F/O McPherson. Cdr. Thompson. Cpl. Arrowsmith.	Photo Reco.	1200.	1650.	Duty successful. 75 photos taken of GERMAN fleet. The first Royal Air Force aircraft to cross the GERMAN frontier.	

Thompson, R.N., acting as Observer, and Corporal Vincent Arrowsmith as Wireless Operator/Air Gunner – had been on stand-by for two days. On that fateful Sunday morning when the long expected War Telegraph, WAR HAS BROKEN OUT WITH GERMANY ONLY, was received by Air Vice-Marshal C.T. Maclean, the A.O.C. of 2 Group, the order was given to make a reconnaissance of the naval port of Wilhelmshaven to locate and photograph vessels of the German fleet that were thought to be leaving the port.

In a mere three days Bomber Command had found that the goalposts had been moved. On 1st September the U.S. President, Franklin D. Roosevelt, had made a direct appeal to Britain, France and Germany to refrain from bombing undefended towns or any targets where civilians might be injured, and both the British and French governments readily gave the necessary assurances, followed 18 days later by Germany. Thus the Command's immediate and sole target was now the German fleet, but only whilst at sea; it was twelfth in the thirteen Western Air Plans that had been formulated in 1938 as the Command's war strategy. Having recently lost the control of the Fleet Air Arm to the Admiralty, it was somewhat galling for the Air Ministry to now find that the R.A.F. was forced to operate at the behest of the Admiralty. Although in retrospect this moratorium proved to be a blessing in disguise, as it afforded the Command some welcome breathing space and more than likely saved aircraft and many precious aircrews.

The Blenheim passed over Wilhelmshaven at an altitude of

A Blenheim observer with a hand-held F24 camera.

21/22,000 ft and so became the first R.A.F. aircraft to cross the German frontier. The crew sighted a number of German warships in the Schillig Roads, which were heading north. Commander Thompson took seventy-five photographs and Corporal Arrowsmith vainly attempted to radio the vital information back to Wyton; because of the intense cold the radio set had frozen! By the time the crew arrived safely back just under five hours later, there was insufficient time to evaluate the intelligence and launch the Command's first bombing raid. The nine crews in each of the three Blenheim squadrons, 107, 110 and 139, were stood down.

Flying Officer Andrew McPherson, D.F.C. (via J. McDonald)

The cameras then used by the R.A.F. were F24s, which dated back to 1925. The main camera was mounted on a steel frame by the emergency hatch door, although often the Observer was also supplied with a hand-held F24 that could be used from the nose of the Blenheim. Although the F24 was a most reliable camera, it was not of a very high definition and was not heated, which caused some technical problems at the operational height of the Blenheims.

The following morning Flying Officer McPherson and his crew were sent out on another reconnaissance sortie of the ports of Wilhelmshaven, Cuxhaven and Brunsbüttel. The weather was appalling – heavy rain and poor visibility – but quite brilliantly McPherson again located enemy vessels at Wilhelmshaven and Brunsbüttel. He flew over them at about 250 ft without being challenged, more photographs were taken, but again all attempts to radio the intelligence back failed, as the coded messages received were unintelligible.

McPherson landed at Wyton at 13.35 hours, and less than an hour later

Loading 250 lb bombs into a Blenheim IV

Bomber Command's Headquarters ordered an immediate low-level attack on the German fleet. Because of the worsening weather conditions, described by one pilot as 'a solid wall of cloud', only five crews from each Blenheim squadron were detailed for the first bombing raid of the war. Their orders were carefully worded: 'The greatest care is to be taken not to injure the civilian population. The intention is to destroy the German Fleet. *There is no alternative target.*'

The five Blenheims of 139 Squadron were the first to leave but the crews were unable to locate the enemy vessels and all returned safely. No 110 from Wattisham, Suffolk, followed about twenty minutes later. Flight Lieutenant Kenneth Doran, who was leading the two squadrons, found the pocket battleship *Admiral von Scheer* and the cruiser *Emden* with what he described as 'an incredible combination of luck and judgement'. Doran's crew made the first attack with three direct hits on the *Admiral von Scheer*, but the 500 lb bombs, which were fitted with eleven-second delay fuses to allow time for the following aircraft to bomb, bounced off the armoured deck and exploded in the sea. The bombs from one of the following Blenheims fell short and another Blenheim was hit by anti-aircraft fire and crashed in flames onto the forecastle of the *Emden,* killing nine German seaman; the four airmen were also killed. Thus Sergeants R. Grossey and S. Otty along with Aircraftsman R. Evans and the pilot, Flying Officer H. Emden sadly became the Command's first fatalities of the war. By a strange quirk of fate, Flying Officer Emden died whilst attacking an enemy vessel bearing his name.

By the time the five crews of 107 Squadron arrived on the scene some minutes later the flak was heavy and accurate, especially from the battleship *Admiral Hipper.* Four aircraft were shot down and all but two of the twelve airmen killed; Sergeant L. Ward and AC1 Slattery became the first of over 9,800 Command crewmen to become prisoners of war. Their Canadian pilot, Sergeant A. Prince, was the first of some 9,900 Canadians to lose their lives whilst serving in Bomber Command; the highest number by far of any Commonwealth country.

It had been a most costly operation with five Blenheims lost along with sixteen brave 'Blenheim Boys', whose war had lasted just a few brief hours. No 3 Group despatched fourteen Wellingtons of 9 and 149 Squadrons from two Suffolk airfields to attack two enemy battleships off Brunsbuttel, but because of the weather conditions the majority turned back or failed to locate their targets, although two from 9 Squadron were shot down by enemy fighters and another ten airmen killed.

Blenheim IV (N6216) of 139 Squadron flew on the first raid – 4th September 1939.
It was shot down on 12th May 1940.

It had been a disastrous day for Bomber Command. Of the twenty-nine aircraft sent out only thirteen crews found their targets and hardly any damage had been sustained by the German vessels, but seven aircraft had been lost along with twenty-six airmen. Furthermore because of a navigation error two bombs were dropped on the Danish town of Esberg, over one hundred miles north of Brunsbüttel, and two people were killed. At a loss rate of 23% it was a bitter blow for the Command's chiefs, which might well presage a most costly autumn for the Command. The *Daily Mail* headlined the news as 'The First Blow' and when *Bomber Command*, the Air Ministry's official booklet, appeared in late 1941, it ignored the tragic loss of so many airmen and commented in rather jingoistic terms on this first raid:

> With this attack the war began. In skill, resource and resolution, it was typical of all which were to follow, and showed clearly to those in command of the Royal Air Force – though they had never doubted that it was so – that the men whose fathers had fought the Germans in the last war were in every way worthy of their begetters.

What was abundantly clear from this first bombing operation was the unflinching courage with which the attacks were pressed home despite strong opposition, which became typical of the Command's aircrews throughout the war.

On 10th September 1939, morale within the Command was lifted somewhat when the first decorations for gallantry were gazetted: D.F.C.s to both Flying Officer McPherson and Flight Lieutenant Kenneth Doran for their actions on the early days of the war. Squadron Leader Doran, D.F.C. & Bar, later went missing on a bombing raid over Stavanger on 30th April 1940, but he

Wellington IC, 'G-LG' of No 215 Squadron at Bassingbourn.

survived as a prisoner of war. Andrew McPherson was killed in action on 12th May 1940 whilst serving in France and Vincent Arrowsmith, the third member of the crew, was killed on 28th September. Such were the heavy casualties suffered in Blenheim squadrons during the first year of the war.

On the operational training front there had been several squadron changes at the two operational training stations. No 63 Squadron left Upwood on 7th September for Abingdon, followed two days later by 52 Squadron to Kidlington. The two squadrons at Bassingbourn, 104 and 108, moved to Bicester on 18th September and on the following day 90 Squadron arrived at Upwood with Blenheim IVs. Pilot Officer T. A. Peele was the first airman to be killed in a flying training accident from Upwood when his Blenheim crashed on 16th October. Although the squadron lost another two aircraft in training accidents there were no other fatalities.

A major change occurred at Bassingbourn on 24th September as the first Vickers Wellingtons appeared in Cambridgeshire when 215 Squadron arrived from Bramcote, Warwickshire. Since October 1935 when the squadron had reformed, it had been equipped with Vickers Virginias, Handley Page Harrows and, from July 1939, Wellingtons. It was now designated a Reserve squadron thus ensuring that Bassingbourn, which had been transferred to 3 Group, would continue to be involved in operational training.

The Vickers Wellington was a most remarkable bomber, beloved by its crews and the public alike. It had been designed by Dr Barnes Wallis, of later 'bouncing bomb' fame, in response to an Air Ministry Specification of October 1935 (B9/32) for a twin-engine heavy bomber. Its unique geodetic lattice construction, which owed much to the design of the R101 airship, proved it could sustain considerable battle damage and still survive; its crews had an abounding faith that their aircraft would bring them home safely despite being severely damaged. Originally called *Crecy* in honour of the famous English victory of 1346, its name was changed to Wellington after the 'Iron Duke'. It later acquired the nickname 'Wimpy' after J. Wellington Wimpy, a character from the popular Popeye newspaper strip cartoon.

The prototype (K4090) first flew on 15th June 1936, production commenced in December 1937 and the first Wellingtons entered the Service in October 1938. One of the squadron's pilots claimed 'they brought a new era of military flying for the pilots of Bomber Command...it was something entirely new and very exciting'. Powered by two Bristol Pegasus XVIII engines, which gave a top speed of about 235 mph at 15,500 ft, it could carry a 4,500 lb bomb load and was the first bomber capable of taking the

4,000 lb 'blockbuster' bomb. There were Frazer-Nash nose and tail turrets with twin .303 inch Browning guns as well as two single Brownings in beam positions.

At the outbreak of war Bomber Command had 175 Wellingtons on charge, mostly with the six operational squadrons in 3 Group. Wellingtons suffered the Command's first heavy losses and in the early war years they formed the backbone of Bomber Command. Over 47,400 operational sorties were made by the Command's forty-five Wellington squadrons (third behind Lancasters and Halifaxes) and some 1,380 (2.9%) Wellingtons were lost in action. Over 11,460 were ultimately built, the largest number of any British bomber, and it became the ubiquitous aircraft at the Command's Operational Training Units; the majority of bomber crews received their operational training on Wellingtons, so the Wimpy held a very special place in the hearts of all 'Bomber Men'.

A Blenheim pilot ready for a flight over the cold North Sea. (via M. Harris)

After No 2 Group's first expensive bombing operation, its tasks were defined as operations against the German Navy and the photo-reconnaissance of enemy communications and troop concentrations in Germany, as well as the twenty-eight airfields in west and north-west Germany. No 114 Squadron returned to Wyton on 15th September 1939 and the two squadrons, alternating between Wyton and Alconbury, became engaged in these operations.

They were dangerous and lonely flights and were undertaken by the crews with great determination and heavy loss. Blenheims were no match for the *Luftwaffe* fighters and also, flying at a relatively low altitude, they became prey to anti-aircraft batteries.

Out of thirty-seven sorties flown from 20th September to 25th November 1939 seven Blenheims were lost – almost 20%. No 139 lost its first crew on 1st October when Flying Officer A.C. MacLaren and his crew failed to return from a photo-reconnaissance flight to Fassberg airfield; he survived as a prisoner of war but his two crewmen were killed. Thirteen days later 114 Squadron lost its first Blenheim in action, thought to have been brought down by a combination of anti-aircraft fire and fighters; the three airmen were killed. On 11th November the squadron suffered a particularly tragic and fatal accident when two of its Blenheims collided in cloud over the Heligoland area and crashed into the sea; the six airmen were killed. The sole surviving Blenheim of the flight returned safely to Wyton to bring the bad news.

At the end of October, No 2 Group's Headquarters moved to Castle Hill House, Huntingdon, where it would remain until June 1943 when the Group left Bomber Command to join the 2nd Tactical Air Force. On 2nd November H.M. King George VI made an official visit to Wyton to conduct the first investiture of the war; he presented the D.F.C.s to Flying Officer MacPherson and Flight Lieutenant Doran. It was the first to be staged 'in the field', yet another milestone for Wyton. His Majesty was accompanied by all the 'top brass' of Bomber Command and as he was a pilot, he showed great interest in examining a Blenheim (N6236) which had been damaged in action on 30th October. Senior Group officers had been greatly surprised at the amount of damage that the aircraft could sustain and still return safely. In the few months of action the Blenheim IV had proved to be a most doughty and pugnacious aircraft, greatly admired by its crews.

In late October it was decided that several Blenheim squadrons would move to join the Advanced Air Striking Force in France to replace some of the Force's Battle squadrons, who would then return to re-equip with Blenheim IVs. Thus 139 was taken off operations on 17th November and moved to Bethenville on 1st December; it was replaced by 40 Squadron. No 114 Squadron was non-operational from 23rd November and left for Conde-Vraux on 9th December. Its replacement was 15 Squadron, better known as 'XV'; the Roman numerals appeared on its badge along with the motto '*Aim Sure*' and it was one of a few R.A.F. squadrons to use such numerals. No XV was one of the oldest operational squadrons, having been formed in 1915, and it would serve continuously throughout the war equipped with five different bombers.

Although the period from September 1939 to April 1940 was dubbed the 'Phoney War' because of a lack of military operations on the ground, it was anything but for Bomber Command. In just four months to the end of December 1939 the Command had been confined to five bombing strikes on units of the German navy, photo-reconnaissance flights and, moreover, dropping millions upon millions of propaganda leaflets over Germany. These 'Nickel' operations, as they were known, had been conducted at night by the Whitley crews of 4 Group. Nevertheless by the end of year the Command had lost seventy aircraft in action and thirteen of these were Blenheims; but more importantly over two hundred and twenty airmen had been killed or were missing in action – all valuable and experienced aircrew. Operational training had also proved costly in men and machines – seventy-nine aircraft written-off and one hundred and six airmen killed.

It had been a harsh introduction into the air war and as yet not a single bomber had crossed into Germany in anger. Judged by these early losses it was obviously going to be a long, hard and costly war for Bomber Command.

An early recruiting poster. (Bomber Command Association)

Chapter 3

By Day and
By Night

(1940)

In many respects 1940 can be considered a year of destiny for the Royal Air Force. During the summer the pilots of Fighter Command faced their greatest challenge and gained a memorable victory over the *Luftwaffe*. Coastal Command, for long the Cinderella of the Service, had begun to develop into a strike force in its own right. The operational training of pilots and crews had been reorganised into a more efficient and effective system, which proved critical in producing a regular supply of highly trained airmen and crews in the years ahead. As far as Bomber Command was concerned, the year ushered in a number of important milestones – the commitment to night operations, the first minelaying operations, the start of its strategic bombing of German industries and Italian targets, the first raid over Berlin, the first time over one hundred bombers were despatched on a single night and, towards the end of the year, the first attack on the centre of a German city, later known as 'area bombing'. All these operations provided the blueprint for its bombing offensive for the rest of the war.

Nevertheless the early months saw little change in the operational pattern, except that Wellington and Hampden squadrons also became engaged in 'Nickel' operations or what the crews called 'confetti throwing'. Over 1,500 *million* leaflets were delivered by crews throughout the war. The daylight operations continued to be undertaken by Blenheim crews of 2 Group and

Blenheim crews in a happy mood!

A carefully posed publicity photograph of a Blenheim IV pilot and observer.

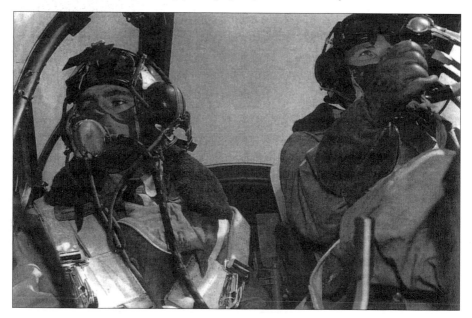

mainly comprised armed reconnaissance sweeps over the North Sea searching for enemy vessels, which according to the Air Ministry at least provided crews with useful formation flying practice! But perhaps the major feature of these months was the severity of the weather – long spells of intense cold and heavy snowfalls; East Anglia suffered its coldest winter since 1881. The harsh weather, which continued well into March, greatly restricted the number of operations both by day and by night. For several weeks during January and February not a single operational sortie was flown.

Despite the atrocious weather conditions operational training continued apace. In pre-war days such training had progressed at a calm and almost leisurely rate but because of aircrew losses and the formation of new squadrons, the courses now demanded that the maximum numbers of trained crews were produced in the minimum amount of time. From February to early April eight airmen were killed in training accidents from the three training squadrons operating from Bassingbourn and Upwood.

Group Commanders had expressed concerns about the standard of crews passing out from the Group Pool Squadrons and one of the first decisions made by Air Marshal Sir Charles 'Peter' Portal when he replaced Ludlow-Hewitt as C-in-C, Bomber Command on 3rd April 1940, was the formation eight Operational Training Units (O.T.U.), thus placing the operational training of crews on a more formal, efficient and hopefully more effective basis. On 8th

Air Marshal Sir Charles 'Peter' Portal was appointed A.O.C.-in-C., Bomber Command in April 1940.
(via J. Adams)

April a radical reorganisation of operational training was introduced with the formation of the first eight O.T.U.s, when 90 and 35 Squadrons at Upwood were disbanded and merged to form 17 O.T.U. and on the same day 11 O.T.U. was formed when 215 Squadron merged with the Station Headquarters at Bassingbourn. All the Units were placed under the control of 6 (Training) Group but on 15th July, an additional Group was formed – No 7 – to cope with the increasing demand for operational training and 17 O.T.U. was transferred into the new Group.

The Units normally comprised four large Flights devoted to all aspects of operational or applied flying training – conversion training, formation flying, navigation, radio communications, aerial armament, practice bombing and fighter affiliation. The intake of crews was normally on a fortnightly basis, with anything from eleven to sixteen crews joining, depending on the size of the Unit. The course was planned to last ten weeks, although this period would vary depending on the time of year. Each intake comprised a larger number of pilots, because at this time bombers carried two pilots, with the other crew categories in equal numbers.

The O.T.U. was the first occasion these aircrew members had come together for training, hitherto they had attended the various specialist units or schools. The most important feature in the early weeks at the Unit was the necessity of the individual categories to form up into a crew. The trainees were herded into a large hangar and told to 'sort themselves out into crews' and were given about seven days to finalise the process. What attracted individuals to crew up ranged from nationality, physical appearance, smoking or drinking habits to sociability. Although this procedure appeared to be rather haphazard and disorganised it nevertheless quite amazingly worked very well. Strong and lasting wartime friendships were forged at this stage of training and those crews fortunate enough to survive an operational tour together remained friends for years ahead. The training would be concentrated on the chosen airmen working together as a team, which was so essential for the effective operation of their aircraft and their ultimate survival.

All forms of flying training were hazardous but operational training posed the greatest risks, and O.T.U.s suffered far higher accident rates than any other type of flying training. In some Units this was as high as 20% over a period of six months. One factor to account for this was youthful and inexperienced crews flying 'aged' aircraft that had been passed down from operational squadrons and therefore were more prone to mechanical failure, especially

The end product of all O.T.U.s: a bomber crew preparing for take-off. An oil painting by Dame Laura Knight, R.A. (Imperial War Museum)

the engines and radio equipment. Also trainee crews were often required to fly in unfavourable weather, and the many and various night-flying exercises presented considerable problems for the inexperienced crews. However, the majority of training accidents were as a result of human error of some description. It should be borne in mind that the young trainee pilots were coping with large and heavy aircraft after only recently mastering the much lighter Airspeed Oxfords.

In the first eight months of operational training there were one hundred and ninety aircraft accidents, of which No 11 O.T.U. lost fourteen Wellingtons and No 17 twenty-eight aircraft, mainly Blenheim IVs. Quite a number were fatal, indeed fifty airmen were killed from the two Units; two were New Zealand airmen and one a Canadian, an early indication of the cosmopolitan nature of the wartime Royal Air Force. Pilot Officer G.M. Farland, killed in a Blenheim IV which crashed near Upwood on 10th May 1940, was the second New Zealand airman lost during operational training; he was one of 1,679 New Zealanders to be killed whilst serving in Bomber Command. Perhaps one of the sobering statistics of Bomber Command was that no less than 8,195 airmen were killed in flying or ground accidents during the war, almost 15% of the Command's total fatalities. It should also be remembered that all these airmen had volunteered for flying duties and the majority of them would not fly a single operational sortie. Moreover this figure was more than double Fighter Command's *total* fatalities during the war.

The arrival of spring heralded the end of the 'Phoney War' and brought in its wake the onslaught of the *Blitzkrieg* and a far different type of air war, which would particularly test the courage and determination of the Blenheim crews to the utmost. For their ordeal by fire during the battle for France, the crews had a new Commander – Air Vice-Marshal James N. Robb, D.S.O., D.F.C. – both awards had been made during the First World War when he was a successful fighter pilot. Just three weeks after his appointment he found that the tactical control of his Group was passed to the Commander of the Advanced Air Striking Force (A.A.S.F.) in France although his squadrons still operated from their U.K. airfields.

Early on 10th May 1940, German troops invaded Holland and Belgium and the seven squadrons of 2 Group were placed on instant readiness. During the following thirty-eight days the Blenheim crews flew over 1,500 sorties and eighty aircraft were lost in action along with two hundred and forty-six airmen; no other R.A.F. Group suffered such grievous losses in a relatively brief period. A number of Squadron and Flight Commanders were lost along with many experienced crewmen and several squadrons were virtually decimated. As Michael Bowyer commented in his admirable history of No 2 Group, 'Its costly contribution to the battle for France was nothing short of heroic; every man who participated was a hero.'

The Group's role in the coming battle had already been clearly delineated: 'To locate the advance of the enemy columns; attack armed fighting vehicles; bomb captured airfields in Holland and Belgium and destroy bridges in the front of the enemy's advance.' The Blenheims operated on or near the battlefield where German fighters were heavily concentrated as indeed were the mobile flak batteries; thus their crews and those of the Battles of the A.A.S.F. suffered horrendous losses in a courageous but utterly futile attempt to stem the enemy's advance.

From the outset XV and 40 Squadrons were engaged in the desperate air battle. Early on the morning of 10th May two Blenheims of 40 Squadron left on a photo-reconnaissance flight over airfields in Holland and Belgium, which were thought to have been captured by enemy paratroopers. Only one crew returned to Wyton; the heavily damaged Blenheim crashed on landing and burst into flames but Squadron Leader Brian Paddon and his crew escaped injury. He was able to report that the airfields were indeed in the enemy's hands.

The missing Blenheim along with Flying Officer R. M. Burns and his crew were the first casualties of the battle. Later in the day nine Blenheims from Alconbury were despatched to bomb Waalhaven airfield, close to Rotterdam, and remarkably all returned safely. Not so the twelve crews of 40 Squadron led by Squadron Leader G.W.C. Gleed and bound for Ypenburg airfield. Three aircraft were shot down and one returned severely damaged with its crew seriously injured: for their courage and determination, the pilot Flight Lieutenant H. Smeddie was awarded the D.F.C. and Sergeant B. Woodbridge and LAC G. Quinn received D.F.M.s.

A Blenheim gunner poses for an official photograph.

Two days later (12th) it was the turn of XV Squadron to suffer when twelve crews were engaged in attacking a bridge at Maastricht. Only six Blenheims returned to Alconbury and all were damaged, leaving the squadron with just two serviceable aircraft. It had virtually been wiped-out; eighteen airmen missing in action and another three seriously injured. Three days later the squadron could provide only three crews to join the nine of 40 Squadron detailed to attack enemy communications and bridges. Another three failed to return, two from No 40, including its Commander, Wing Commander Ernest Barlow, and one from XV.

The mayhem continued three days later when XV lost another three aircraft in action whilst attacking enemy forces at Le Cateau; all of the pilots were Flight or Sector leaders – Squadron Leader Hector Lawrence,

Flying Officer F. Dawson-Jones and Flight Lieutenant P. Chapman. Three Blenheims landed at Abbeville airfield as the pilots judged that they were too damaged to fly back to Wyton. However, one piloted by Flying Officer Leonard Trent did manage to get back to Martlesham Heath; Trent, a New Zealander, would be awarded the Victoria Cross in May 1943 whilst serving with 487 (NZ) Squadron.

Air Marshal Portal expressed his deep concern at the Group's losses: 'The operations in France are draining away the Blenheim crews at the rate of 1 or 2 squadrons per week…It is the height of unwisdom [sic] to throw Blenheims away in an attempt to do the work of artillery.' The Air Staff decided that in future Blenheims would operate by night, though the crews had no experience of night flying. However, when Air Marshal Barratt of the A.A.S.F. called for urgent assistance it was reluctantly agreed that daylight operations would continue, but only with fighter escorts. The Chief of the Air Staff, Air Chief Marshal Sir Cyril Newall, passed a message to 2 Group:

> Please convey to the pilots and crews of your Group my congratulations and admiration on the manner in which they have carried out the tasks allotted to them in the present operation. Their determination and success have earned unstinted praise from our Allies, and reflect the greatest credit on all concerned.

During May the air war changed for the other crews of Bomber Command. On the 15th the *Luftwaffe* bombed Rotterdam and almost 1,000 Dutch civilians were killed. The immediate reaction of the War Cabinet was to authorise bombers to cross the Rhine and bomb German industrial targets. On the night of the 15th/16th ninety-nine aircraft were despatched to sixteen industrial targets in the Ruhr valley: the Command's strategic bombing offensive had begun, without doubt 'the gloves were now off'. Almost one month later, after Italy's entry into the war, both Genoa and Turin were bombed by Whitleys of 4 Group. Over the coming months an increasing number of industrial targets in north-west Germany were attacked by night, at least as and when the battle for France allowed.

By 23rd May Blenheim losses had been so heavy that the Group had only sixty serviceable aircraft, probably equivalent to just four squadrons. On this day 40 Squadron lost two aircraft, along with one from XV, when attacking enemy troops near Arras. Amongst the missing airmen was

Wing Commander J. Llewellyn, 40's Squadron Commander; his observer, Pilot Officer William Edwards, was the first of three brothers to be killed in Blenheims during the war. The squadron had lost its second Commander within eight days.

So many pre-war pilots had been lost over the previous thirteen days, and many of the missing observers and air gunners were highly skilled tradesmen, most of them trained at Halton. The loss of such experienced airmen, along with many fine squadron and flight leaders, was a heavy blow for the Group; they were irreplaceable. During the month, the two squadrons had lost twenty-six Blenheims in action and sixty-three airmen killed. One airman serving at Wyton during those days, later recalled: 'Everyone I met at that time was a hero and I think most of us were very frightened, although very few showed it. They were very bad times.' Sadly, matters were not going to improve.

For a brief period during late May and early June 1940 another Blenheim squadron operated from Wyton, No 57, one of the two Blenheim squadrons

A Radio Operator.

serving in France as the Air Component of the British Expeditionary Force. From 26th May until 3rd June the Blenheim crews attacked enemy troop positions around Dunkirk as their contribution to Operation *Dynamo*. On the following day the Air Staff issued a directive to the Group Commander: 'It is essential that the destructive efforts of our night bombing operations over Germany should be continued by daylight operations on the same objectives, only when cloud cover gives adequate security.' Although for most of June, Blenheim operations were concentrated on airfields in the occupied countries with the occasional foray into Germany.

During June there were also a number of operations attacking German troops in northern France, and one such raid on the 6th proved very costly for 40 Squadron. Twelve crews left Wyton to bomb German troop positions close to St Valéry where the 51st Highland Division was still valiantly holding out. Five aircraft failed to return and of the fifteen airmen, three were killed. Three evaded capture and returned to the United Kingdom; one, Sergeant B. Baker, an air gunner, was taken to a French hospital but despite his injuries he managed to escape via Brittany. The other eight airmen were made prisoners of war, including the leader of the operation, Squadron Leader Brian Paddon, who was then the squadron's most experienced airman and leader.

It seemed that Paddon, like so many other captured airmen, was hell-bent on escaping and by 1941 he had been sent to Colditz Castle or *Oflag* IV.C, which was the camp for *ausbrecher* or inveterate escapers. He made an unsuccessful escape attempt from there whilst being treated in a military hospital at nearby Dresden. In June 1942 Paddon was sent to Stalag-Luft XX.A at Thorn in Poland, where he was to face a court-martial for 'insulting a German NCO'. After only a day in Thorn he managed to escape and completed a 150 mile journey to the port of Stettin, where he was taken on board a Swedish vessel and within a week had safely arrived in Sweden. Paddon's nickname whilst in prison was 'Never-a-dull-moment', which seemed to be well earned. When he finally arrived back in the United Kingdom in August Paddon was awarded a D.S.O.; he was the fourth airman to arrive back safely from captivity.

In June 1940 both squadrons lost experienced Flight Commanders: Squadron Leader W. Burke and his crew of XV Squadron went missing on the 8th when attacking an airfield at Poix and six days later Squadron Leader G.W.C. Gleed, along with another crew of 40 Squadron, failed to return after attacking enemy troops near Fresney. After the fall of France

Invasion barges in the port of Dunkirk in the late summer of 1940.

the Group's Blenheims were engaged in attacking enemy airfields as well as ports in Holland, Belgium and northern France as a large armada of sea-going barges was assembling for the proposed invasion of the United Kingdom. These operations were mainly conducted by night, although the aircraft were not properly equipped for such operations.

When Oakington opened on 1st July, it was one of the last pre-war Expansion stations planned for Cambridgeshire. Construction work had started in the summer of 1939 but because of the outbreak of war a limit was imposed on the number of permanent buildings and hangars and perhaps needless to say the airfield was grass covered, no hard runways had been laid.

Blenheim IVs of No 40 Squadron at Wyton – Summer 1940. (Imperial War Museum)

Until all the buildings were completed in the autumn many of the airmen lived under canvas and the officers' and sergeants' messes were housed in large marquees. The new station was situated about five miles north-east of Cambridge between the villages of Oakington and Longstanton.

Seventeen days later 218 Squadron arrived from Mildenhall, Suffolk. It had served with the A.A.S.F. in France since February 1940 and had experienced a most torrid time, losing thirteen Battles in action before being evacuated on 13th June. The crews were now converting to Blenheim IVs and unfortunately seven airmen were killed on 18th August when two aircraft collided whilst engaged in training. Four days later, on the 22nd/23rd, the first Blenheim was lost in action after a mission to Bruges and Squadron Leader C.C. House was killed.

Meanwhile the 'old stagers' at Wyton and Alconbury were largely operating by night; although perhaps 'old stagers' was not strictly correct as so many new crews had been posted into the two squadrons. As one airman later recalled, 'they came to us like boys with little operational training but they soon became men'. On 17th/18th July one of the 'old stagers', Squadron Leader Webster of XV Squadron made the first intruder raid of the war when he made a low-level attack on Caen airfield, the forerunner of thousands of such raids in the coming years. Five nights later (25th/26th) both squadrons were engaged in the Command's largest operation of the war so far; one hundred and sixty-six bombers despatched to seven targets in the Ruhr and airfields in Holland. Only two Blenheims were lost, one from each squadron. One crew was captured and some forty years later Sergeant Roger Peacock wrote about his experiences with 40 Squadron;

his book, *Blenheim Boy*, under the pen name of Richard Passmore, was published in 1981.

The 'Blenheim Boys' contribution to the Battle of Britain was acknowledged in Winston Churchill's famous speech of 20th August: 'Never in the field of human conflict was so much owed by some many to so few...', although his fulsome appreciation of the Blenheim crews is rarely quoted:

> On no part of the Royal Air Force does the weight of the war fall more heavily than on the daylight bombers, who play an invaluable part in the case of an invasion and whose unfailing zeal it has been necessary in the meantime on numerous occasions to restrain.

The first attack on invasion barges had taken place on 3rd July but during September 1940 Blenheim crews, along with the heavy bombers, were engaged in an intensive night offensive against barges berthed in the Channel ports and those along the Belgian and Dutch coasts. For thirteen consecutive nights from 13th/14th September Command crews flew over 1,000 sorties – their contribution to the Battle of Britain. Fortunately the losses were relatively slight; XV and 40 Squadrons each lost one crew. It

Winston Churchill at Oakington watching Stirling 'D-Dog' of 7 Squadron setting out on a 'shattering strike of retributive justice'. (via L. Norman)

was subsequently reported that three hundred and sixty barges had been destroyed. By the end of September when the threat of invasion had passed, at least temporarily, there was a dilemma for the Air Staff as to the future role for the eleven Blenheim squadrons and it was decided that four were to be equipped with Wellingtons.

By the beginning of November the three Blenheim squadrons operating in Cambridgeshire were transferred to 3 Group and began to exchange their Blenheims for Wellington 1Cs, although 218 Squadron moved from Oakington to Marham, and 57 Squadron, which had returned to Wyton after operating in Scotland, would convert to Wellingtons at Feltwell. During the time that XV and 40 Squadrons had been operating from Wyton and Alconbury they had each lost twenty-nine Blenheims in action and almost the same number of airmen – seventy-two and seventy-three respectively. It was not until mid-December that both squadrons were operational with their Wellingtons; on 21st/22nd December crews of XV Squadron bombed Bremen whilst No 40 attacked Antwerp, all returning safely.

In late October 1940 Oakington had suddenly become the focus of intense interest when the first Short Stirlings landed from Leeming; No 7 Squadron had arrived and it was destined to remain at Oakington for the rest of the war. As its number suggests the squadron was one the oldest in the Service, originally formed in May 1914. In July 1940 it had reformed at Leeming specifically to introduce the Stirling into operations and was commanded by Wing Commander Paul Harris, who had completed an operational tour with 149 Squadron flying Wellingtons.

The Stirling was the first four-engine bomber to enter Bomber Command, one of the series of heavy bombers designed to the Air Ministry's famous specification B12/36, which really dictated the format of the Command's wartime heavy bomber force. The prototype had first flown in May 1939 but

Wellingtons of No 40 Squadron at Alconbury.

Short Stirling being 'bombed-up'.

unfortunately it crashed on landing, which delayed the testing programme. Nevertheless the first production Stirling (L7605) appeared exactly twelve months later. There had never been another aeroplane quite like the Stirling. Compared with the Lancaster and Halifax it was the tallest (22 ft 9 inches from ground to cockpit), the longest at 87 ft and with the shortest wingspan at 99 ft, specifically limited to be housed in the pre-war hangars!

The aircraft looked ungainly on the ground and, at first sight, could be rather daunting to new crews; it appeared to be a giant compared with the Hampden and Wellington. In flight it proved to be highly manoeuvrable, gaining the name, 'fighter bomber', and not solely because of the eight .303 machine guns in its three turrets; by repute it could turn inside a Spitfire. It was a most sturdy aircraft, able to sustain considerable damage and with a maximum bomb load of 14,000 lbs over a range of some 740 miles, capable of delivering what Winston Churchill called 'the shattering strikes of retributive justice'. But with a cruising speed of 200 mph and a relatively low operational height of 10,000-12,000 ft, it suffered proportionally higher losses than both the Lancaster and Halifax. Air Marshal Harris had a poor opinion of the aircraft although it served his Command well; during 1943 twelve Stirling squadrons operated in 3 Group. They later operated as transports, glider towers and troop carriers and over 2,730 were produced in various marks.

Even by late December 1940 7 Squadron had just five Stirlings on charge and all were training aircraft; the first operational aircraft was not received until the following January. The Stirling was not easy to produce and there had been certain production problems, which allied to the bombing of Shorts' factories at Rochester and Belfast delayed its entry into the air war. It had also introduced a new crew member – flight engineer – who monitored the performance of the engines and generally assisted the captain. As yet there was no specialist training in place for the new aircrew member, so the squadron proceeded to train suitably qualified ground staff, which only further delayed its operational readiness.

Bomber Command now had a new Commander, Air Marshal Sir Richard Peirse, who had taken over from Sir Charles Portal on 5th October. Sir Charles was appointed Chief of the Air Staff and as such retained a strong and powerful influence on the Command's progress throughout the war. General Ismay, Churchill's right-hand man, said of Portal, 'he was the best of all war leaders – quite easily'. He was created a Viscount in 1946 and his statue stands outside the Ministry of Defence buildings in London.

Peirse had taken charge of some five hundred and thirty serviceable bombers but almost a half (two hundred and seventeen) were Blenheims and another eighty-five were Battles, which were soon withdrawn from the Command. Furthermore the remaining Hampdens and Whitleys were due to be phased out in favour of the new bombers. For its major task ahead – the night bombing of Germany – the Command was left with about one hundred and fifty bombers, mainly Wellingtons.

Thus as the first complete year of the war came to an end, Bomber Command was really not much stronger than it had been in January 1940. It had been a hard twelve months during which seven hundred and sixty-two aircraft had been lost in action and another one hundred and ten in accidents. Over 2,540 airmen were missing in action; the majority were sergeants, many of whom had entered the Service via the Volunteer Reserve. Besides this heavy loss of life, another deep concern for the Command was the number of senior and experienced leaders that had been lost, no less than fifty-one Squadron Leaders and eleven Wing Commanders. Nevertheless it had, at least, started its long and bitter strategic bombing offensive.

Chapter 4

A Hard Lesson

(1941)

Cambridgeshire's three operational squadrons, 7, XV and 40, now operated in 3 Group, which had been commanded by Air Vice-Marshal John 'Jack' Baldwin since the outbreak of war. He was a popular commander and occasionally flew operations with his crews, a practice actively discouraged by Command headquarters.

The Group's motto, *Nothing without Labour,* certainly proved apposite for its operations during 1941. It was a costly and traumatic twelve months for the Command and its crews and, in many ways, a frustrating one. During the year a number of directives was issued, which every few months changed its priorities from its planned campaign – the strategic bombing of Germany's industries. Perhaps most notable was the number of occasions it was called upon to attack the German vessels, *Scharnhorst, Gneisenau* and *Prinz Eugen,* whilst they were in the French Atlantic ports. Sir Charles Portal was less than happy with this diversion of his bomber force and considered it a matter of 'getting the Admiralty out of its mess'! Furthermore, before the year was out, the Command's future role was under close and serious debate and the fate of its strategic bombing offensive was seriously in doubt.

Nevertheless there was a positive start to the year when on the first three nights of January Bremen was bombed, followed in the middle of the month by two heavy raids on Wilhelmshaven, where the battleship *Tirpitz* was

A deadly tracery of flak over Brest in 1941.

berthed, the first of many attempts to destroy this vessel over the coming years. According to German sources the first raid on Wilhelmshaven on the 15th/16th was very effective: 'The year of 1941 would bring more heavy raids but none causing such heavy damage as this one.' The following night's operation was not so successful, few crews found the target and five of the eighty-one aircraft were lost (6%). One of the missing aircraft was from 40 Squadron, their first Wellington lost in action; the six airmen were all sergeants, an all-British crew, as were the majority of crews during most of 1941.

The first directive was issued on 15th January, when Air Marshal Peirse was instructed that 'the sole and primary aim of your bomber offensive should be the destruction of the German synthetic oil plants'; seventeen targets were listed, names that would figure large in the Command's offensive over the next three years. A month later (15th/16th February) XV Squadron lost their first Wellington in action whilst attacking one of these targets – the Holten oil plant at Sterkrade. It was shot down by a night fighter; two of the crew survived as prisoners of war.

On 11th January 1941 a new airfield had opened at Waterbeach, six miles north-east of Cambridge alongside the A10 road to Ely, one of the last Expansion stations. The airfield was blessed with good drainage and suffered less from mud and surface water than others in the county. It was also provided with hard runways unlike the other operational airfields. In this respect Oakington was suffering particularly badly, where the heavy Stirlings had turned the airfield into a quagmire; the pre-war decision not to provide concrete runways for its new bomber stations was coming home to roost. In March, the Under-Secretary State for Air, Harold Balfour, remarked, 'I tried today to fly to Oakington but found it impossible to land there because the aerodrome is unserviceable...there we are with the first Stirlings, but they are unable to function normally because of an untracked base!'

Aside from the state of the airfield, there were several technical problems with the Stirlings and the supply was rather slow, so it was not until 10th/11th February that No 7 was able to mount its first operational sorties, when just three bombed oil storage tanks at Rotterdam. A fortnight later (24th/25th) three Stirlings joined the main force attacking warships in Brest. It was over this target on 3rd/4th March that the first Stirling was lost in action. It crashed in the English Channel and the missing eight-man crew included Squadron Leader J.M. Griffith-Jones, D.F.C., an experienced Flight Commander. Coincidentally another new four-engine bomber – the Handley Page Halifax – made its first appearance during the month.

Early in March 1941 the Command's priorities changed when Winston Churchill ordered: 'We must take the offensive against the U-boat and the Focke-Wulf whenever we can and wherever we can. The U-boat at sea must be hunted, the U-boat in the building yard or in dock must be bombed. The Focke-Wulf Condor and other bombers employed against our shipping must be attacked in the air and in their nests.' Thus the U-boat yards at Kiel, Hamburg, Bremen and Vegesack became familiar targets, as did the Focke-

Wellington (R1013) of 40 Squadron shot down over Berlin 12th/13th March 1941. Squadron Leader E. Hugh Lynch-Bosse and his crew baled out. (via M. R. Lawrence)

Wulf factories along with the U-boat bases at Lorient, St Nazaire, Brest and Bordeaux.

Nevertheless the first major raid on Berlin in 1941 was mounted on the night of 12th/13th March, but the bombing was very scattered with little damage sustained. A Wellington of 40 Squadron piloted by Squadron Leader E. Hugh Lynch-Bosse was shot down; all the crew baled out and were taken prisoner. Lynch-Bosse was taken to 'L3' at Sagan, the most celebrated P.O.W. camp. Years later he recalled that this had occurred on the 13th whilst he was on his 13th mission in Wellington R1013, although he claimed that he was not superstitious! Like many senior officers who went missing during 1941, Lynch-Bosse was a pre-war regular officer and Cranwell graduate. At Oakington another Squadron Leader Lynch-Bosse – 'P.W.' – was a Flight Commander with 7 Squadron.

On the same night 40 Squadron lost another crew, who were on their first operational sortie to Boulogne. It was then normal procedure to send 'freshmen' crews to what were considered 'easy' targets. All six airmen were killed; their average age was just twenty years. It had also become an established practice to send trainee crews on Nickel operations over occupied countries as they were nearing the end of their courses; it was maintained that these operations provided 'valuable operational experience' but they also resulted in a considerable number of fatalities.

As the Command's losses steadily mounted, the demand for replacement crews became more urgent and the operational training courses were reduced by two weeks, which meant that night flying exercises were undertaken when really weather conditions were far from suitable and resulted in far more accidents. The importance of operational training cannot be overstated; the continual and regular supply of trained crews would prove critical to the outcome of the air war over Europe from 1942 onwards.

In March one of the Group's premier squadrons, 99 (Madras Presidency), arrived at Waterbeach from Newmarket Heath, where it had been operating since the outbreak of the war. The squadron had been the first to receive Wellingtons back in October 1938. At the end of the month its crews were engaged over Brest an attempt to sink the *Scharnhorst* and *Gneisenau*, which had been exacting a heavy toll of British shipping in the Atlantic; because they figured so frequently as targets, the crews had nicknamed them *Salmon* and *Gluckstein* (from the name of a well-known chain of tobacconists) although the official code-name was *Toads*!

Pilot Officer William Dixon, D.F.C. (on the left) and his crew of 99 Squadron – April 1941.

On 3rd/4th April 1941, the third of four nights when Brest had been targeted, Pilot Officer William Dixon of 99 Squadron was awarded an 'immediate' D.F.C. for his part in the operation. The citation concluded: 'This officer has shown the most praiseworthy courage and determination and is an exceptional pilot and captain of an aircraft.' Such was the concern that the Prime Minister felt about the Battle of the Atlantic, that he telephoned the Station Commander at Waterbeach and told him, 'See the lad [Dixon] puts up his D.F.C. ribbon this day.' Dixon was only twenty years old and had entered the R.A.F. in 1939. By 1943 he would have completed a second operational tour flying Halifaxes and been awarded the D.S.O. for 'displaying an absolute determination to complete his allotted tasks'. He retired from the Service in 1975 as a Group Captain. Dixon was just one of many, many brave young men – the 'unsung' heroes – that flew with the Command during 1941, such was the high calibre of its crews.

No 99 Squadron lost its first crews in action on 9th/10th April; Squadron Leader D.C. Torrens and his crew went missing on a raid to Berlin but all survived as prisoners of war. Torrens was somewhat unusual in Bomber Command at that time as he was an ex-fighter pilot who had converted to bombers. Ten nights later another of its Wellingtons, returning from Cologne, collided with a barrage balloon cable over Harwich harbour; it burst into flames and crashed into the sea just offshore, with a complete loss of life. This tragic incident illustrates yet another nightly hazard faced by the crews. To have survived enemy flak and night fighters only to crash within sight of England seemed especially cruel.

As the production of Stirlings improved, it was decided to equip XV Squadron with the new bomber and the first appeared at Wyton on 11th April; by the end of the month the first sorties were mounted, a most commendable effort by Squadron Commander, Wing Commander H.R. Dale, ably assisted by his two Flight Commanders – Squadron Leaders Menaul and Morris. Rather ambitiously, four were despatched to Berlin on the 30th and Flight Lieutenant Raymond joined his three senior officers. For various reasons his aircraft was the only one to reach Berlin. Ten nights later (the 10th/11th) two returned to Berlin – captained by Wing Commander Dale and Flight Lieutenant Raymond – but only one returned to Wyton. Wing Commander Dale's Stirling was shot down by a night fighter and all seven crewmen were killed; Wing Commander P.B.B. Oglivie took over the command of the squadron.

During April there was a change of commander in the other Stirling

Stirling 'LS-J' of No XV Squadron.

squadron, which brought one of the most charismatic and legendary leaders of Bomber Command – Wing Commander H. Robert Graham, D.S.O., D.F.C. He was an excellent pilot, in fact 'the best pilot in Bomber Command' as he was described by the *Daily Express*. He was known affectionately to his airmen as '*der Fuhrer*' or more often

Wing Commander H. Robert Graham, D.S.O., D.F.C., Commander of 7 Squadron – 'the best pilot in Bomber Command' according to the Daily Express.

51

as plain 'Bob'. Graham had already completed an operational tour with 99 Squadron and he remained at Oakington for a year, when he was promoted to Group Captain. He survived the war and finally left the Service as an Air Commodore.

From April onwards there was a deadly menace lurking in the night skies over Cambridgeshire – Junkers 88Cs of the NJG2 (*Nachtjager*) of the German night intruder force. The first aircraft to fall to NJG2 was a Wellington of 11 O.T.U., which was shot down on the night of 10th April. Two weeks later another of the Unit's Wellingtons was severely damaged whilst engaged in practice night circuits over Bassingbourn. After these incidents every training Wellington carried a gunner in the rear turret. The threat of aerial attack placed even greater strain on the trainee crews. A total of twelve aircraft were shot down over Cambridgeshire. Most were training aircraft but two operational aircraft were damaged and crashed on their return from night operations; another additional hazard for the exhausted crews to face when they were so close to their airfield. During the summer several airfields were bombed; on 13th August ten airmen were killed and another twelve injured in a raid on Bassingbourn. Rather mercifully, in early October, NJG2 was moved to Sicily on the direct orders of Hitler.

During the summer of 1941 the Command's losses began to mount steadily, from 3.9% in May to 7% in August, when 5% was really considered as the maximum 'tolerable' casualty rate; although even this figure would seriously impinge on the planned expansion of the Command. Many of the losses were as a result of the greatly strengthened German night fighter force; by mid-July over one hundred and forty night fighters were based mainly in Holland.

There was also a positive change in the enemy's fighter tactics. Hitherto the technique had been to find the R.A.F. bombers in searchlight beams over the targets but the heavy flak had prevented the night fighters engaging the bombers. Now the German Commander, Josef Kammhuber, had established a continuous belt of searchlights directly behind the coast from Denmark to Holland, these allied to a chain of 'boxes' – areas of the skies where the night fighters could be controlled from the ground – and the provision of airborne radar sets made the Kammhuber Belt a most formidable obstacle for the crews. It was claimed that the number of bombers shot down by night fighters increased from forty-two in 1940 to four hundred and twenty-one in 1941. Long gone were the days when an airmen finishing his tour of thirty operations could claim, 'I saw plenty of flak but never saw any night fighters.'

July was a particularly harsh month for the Command, with one hundred and eighty-seven aircraft lost in action along with seven hundred and eighty airmen; of these nearly a quarter were officers including a Group Captain, four Wing Commanders and thirteen Squadron Leaders, all experienced airmen and fine leaders. The squadrons operating from Cambridgeshire airfields lost in total twenty aircraft (eleven Stirlings and nine Wellingtons). Early in the month (9th) a new directive was received by Bomber Command:

> I am directed to inform you that a comprehensive review of the enemy's present political, economic and military situation discloses that the weakest points in his armour lie in the morale of the civil population and in his inland transportation system…you will direct the main effort of the bomber force until further instructions, towards dislocating the German transportation system and *to destroying the morale of the civil population as a whole and of the industrial workers in particular.* (my italics)

Thus 'area bombing', perhaps the most contentious aspect of the Command's bombing offensive, had been authorised by the War Cabinet at such an early juncture.

For just over two weeks during July the heavy bomber crews became involved in the very unpopular 'Circus' operations. These were effectively daylight raids over northern France with fighter escorts with the intention of drawing the *Luftwaffe* fighters into the air, in order to occupy them and so prevent their redeployment on the Eastern Front. With some justification the crews felt that they were being used as live bait, although the Blenheim crews of 2 Group had been engaged on such operations since January.

In the midst of such mayhem there was an incident of black humour. On 14th/15th July a Stirling of 7 Squadron returning with heavy damage from Hanover ran out of fuel and the crew abandoned their aircraft near Northampton; tragically the pilot, Flight Sergeant B.K. Madgewick, slipped out of his parachute harness and fell to his death, but the rest of the crew survived. The aircraft eventually crashed onto Gold Street in the centre of Northampton causing considerable damage to commercial properties but no loss of civilian lives. The Chief Constable of Northamptonshire telephoned the Station Commander to protest in the strongest terms; he is reported to have said, 'I can't have this happening in my county!'

Many anxious hours were spent on the control tower waiting for the returning crews.

Also on the same night another Stirling was abandoned seven miles south of Norwich; all the crew baled out safely and thus another celebrated hero of Bomber Command survived. The pilot, Flying Officer Dennis T. Witt, D.F.M., had joined 7 Squadron in November 1940 as a newly commissioned officer after completing an operational tour on Whitleys with 10 Squadron. Witt finished his second tour with 7 Squadron and by March 1944 he would have completed one hundred operational missions, over a third of them with the Pathfinders; few airmen exceeded this record. In 1945 he was awarded a D.S.O. for 'the highest standard of skill and bravery setting an example of a high order'. He retired from the R.A.F. in 1959 as a Group Captain and died five years later at the age of forty-eight.

Flying Officer Witt was just one of the many fine pilots serving with

No 7 Squadron. Another was Flight Lieutenant George B. Blacklock, D.F.M.; he also was awarded an 'immediate' D.F.C. after a raid to Bremen on 28th June. He had entered the pre-war Service as an apprentice at Halton and had already completed an operational tour on Wellingtons with 99 Squadron. He was then chosen as one of three pilots for the Stirling Development Flight before becoming one of the original members of the reformed No 7 Squadron and the first captain of a four-engine bomber. Blacklock completed a second operational tour with 7 Squadron and retired from the Service in 1961 as a Group Captain. He was a fine example of one of the very many 'Halton or Trenchard brats' that made such a contribution to the Command's aircrews.

The second airfield to open in Cambridgeshire during 1941 was sited at Bourn, about seven miles west of Cambridge and to the south of the A45 road. It had been built during 1940/1 and was a typical wartime airfield with three concrete runways, planned as a satellite for Oakington. In late July, 101 Squadron, which had moved into Oakington earlier in the month, began to use Bourn on a temporary basis until it moved permanently there in 1942. In August another airfield opened at Warboys about seven miles south-west of Chatteris and was originally intended to act as a satellite for 17 O.T.U. at Upwood but soon it was being used by Stirlings of XV Squadron, more especially later in the year when concrete runways were being laid at Wyton. It was nearly a year before an operational squadron was permanently based there.

The men of Bomber Command were held in high regard and esteem by the British public, who had bravely and valiantly lived through the horrendous blitzes of the winter of 1940/41 – after all, it was the only military force that was striking back at the enemy. The daily radio bulletins of bombers attacking German targets were eagerly awaited. In July a fifty-minute feature film, *Target for Tonight*, directed by Harry Watt, was released; it became an immediate popular success and one of the most celebrated documentaries of the war. The public warmed to the crew of the Wellington, *F for Freddie*, sent against a target in the Ruhr. The Wellington pilot, 'Squadron Leader Dixon', was actually Squadron Leader Charles 'Percy' Pickard, D.S.O., D.F.C., and he was destined to become one of the famous 'heroes' of Bomber Command; as a Group Captain he was killed leading the famous Mosquito raid on Amiens prison in February 1944. He was described as 'one of the great airmen of the war'.

Certainly neither the public nor indeed the crews were aware of the damning report of the inadequacies of the bombing offensive, which was in the hands of the War Cabinet in August 1941. The famous Butt Report had been compiled by D.M. Butt of the War Cabinet Secretariat on behalf of Lord Cherwell, the Prime Minister's scientific adviser. Butt had analysed over 4,000 aerial photographs taken in one hundred night raids during June and July. They revealed that only one in four crews that had claimed to have bombed the target had actually been within five miles of it. Over the Ruhr valley where intense flak and industrial haze affected the bombing, the figure fell alarmingly to one crew in ten. Furthermore, as the precious cameras were only issued to more experienced crews, the situation was even more serious. It was known from debriefings that on average one third of all crews did not claim to have actually reached the target area for a variety of reasons. With mounting losses and faced with such evidence the future of the Command's strategic bombing offensive looked rather bleak.

However, it is possible that a number of crews were aware of the inaccuracy of the navigation and bombing, and one pilot in particular, Pilot Officer W. David C. Hardie of 101 Squadron, kept a diary in which he expressed his misgivings: 'The majority of crews are shooting a hell of a line when they get back from a trip...From

Official photograph of a rear gunner in 1941 – 1. Helmet; 2. Oxygen mask/microphone; 3. Oxygen tube; 4. Intercom lead; 5. Dog-clips for chest-type parachute; 6. Mae West life-jacket; 7. Tapes for Mae West; 8. Quick release for harness; 9. Parachute-harness webbing; 10. Lambs wool lining to leather flying jacket.

Rear gunner's 'office' on a Wellington.

my experience I would think that night bombing, unless on a heavy and prolonged scale, is unlikely to yield very few important results.' Sadly Hardie would not live long enough to see this happen, he and his crew ditched off the Dutch coast on 7th/8th November after the ill-fated Berlin operation and none survived.

During September 1941, despite mounting losses, over one hundred and fifty bombers were despatched on twelve nights to various targets in Germany and Italy. In total over 3,000 sorties were made during the month for the loss of one hundred and fifty aircraft or 4.9%, which was only just within the 'tolerable' limit, although on several nights the loss rate was far higher. For instance on the 28th/29th when Frankfurt was the major target, ten out of ninety-two aircraft were lost (10.8%) and of these, four Wellington crews came from 99 Squadron; one crew comprised two New Zealanders, a Canadian and an Australian. Of the twenty-one airmen missing on the night all but two were sergeants. Three airmen managed to evade capture. But perhaps one of the most famous evaders and escapees started his colourful adventures during September.

Sergeant Richard B. Pape was a navigator with XV Squadron; his Stirling was shot down over Holland on 7th/8th September when returning from Berlin. Over the next few years he spent his time evading capture and escaping from POW camps. Pape was tortured and almost three years to the day after he was shot down he was repatriated on health grounds. In

Flying Officer Peter J. S. Boggis in the cockpit of Stirling (N6086) MacRobert's Reply *of XV Squadron – October 1941.*

1952 he described his experiences in his book *Boldness Be My Friend.* All evaders and escapees required the utmost courage, great determination and considerable resolve and, of course, assistance from hundreds of brave people in the occupied countries.

It was during September that perhaps the most famous Stirling of the war began operating with XV Squadron at Wyton – *MacRobert's Reply.* Lady MacRobert, who had lost three sons in flying accidents (two in the R.A.F.), provided £20,000 for the cost of a Stirling – N6086/LS-F. It carried the emblem of the MacRobert family along with its name. For most of its twelve operational sorties it was flown by Flying Officer Peter J.S. Boggis. The aircraft was damaged at Lossiemouth whilst on detachment and after repair it was later used for conversion training at Waterbeach until it crashed near Oakington in March 1943. Meanwhile its replacement – W7531 – was shot down by flak on 17th May 1942 killing its pilot, Squadron Leader J.C. Hall, D.F.C., MiD., and his seven-man crew.

The Command's reputation was further burnished when, in October, the Air Ministry published *Bomber Command*, a booklet of persuasive text and excellent photographs describing its bombing offensive up to July 1941. One might argue that the tone of the booklet was rather jingoistic and that it exaggerated the effectiveness of the bombing offensive, certainly in the light of the Butt Report. However, it was unstinting in its praise of the bomber crews; they were likened to that breed of men who sailed in the *Golden Hind* and accompanied Captain Scott in Antarctica and were described thus:

> These twentieth-century 'gentlemen of the shade, minions of the moon', have accomplished much in twenty-two months of war. Their hearts are high. They have learnt skill and resource flying in aircraft, which, when the war began, were the finest of their kind. Now new types of greater power are in their hands bearing new bombs of more deadly fashioning. By day they will go out in these new aircraft with their comrades of Fighter Command even farther into the confines of the foe. By night they

A Wellington crew entering their aircraft – 'Gentlemen of the shade, minions of the moon'.

The booklet Bomber Command *was published in October 1941.*

will take them 'aloft incumbent on the dusky air' to the farthest town and city of Germany. No chosen target can escape them. The Germans are waging war as they have always waged it: without mercy, respite or limit, with no regard to place or person. Perhaps they may regret the consequences. Perhaps they are already doing so. One thing is certain. Bomber Command will allow no pause, no breathing space. Our attack will go on, fierce because it is relentless, deadly because it is sure.

In October 1941, 40 Squadron was informed that two Flights were to be sent to serve in Malta, purely as an 'emergency detachment'. But before the final orders were received the squadron lost four crews in two operations. On the 14th/15th, when Nuremberg was the target for eighty aircraft, icing and thick cloud severely effected the bombing. Only fourteen crews actually bombed the selected target and four Wellingtons failed to return; eighteen of the squadron's airmen did not return to Alconbury, including Sergeant

B. C. Dynott, who at the age of forty-one was thought to be one of the oldest members of aircrew.

Two nights later another crew was lost over Duisburg and the pilot, Squadron Leader T.G. Kirby-Green was the only survivor as a prisoner. His capture was considered such a coup that it was even announced on the German radio by 'Lord Haw Haw' (William Joyce). Kirby-Green was one of the fifty R.A.F. officers executed on Hitler's direct orders on 29th March 1944 after 'The Great Escape' from *Stalag-Luft* III. Also serving on the squadron at this time was another pilot, Sergeant H. 'Ken' Rees, who also participated in 'The Great Escape' and although recaptured he survived. He remained in the R.A.F. after the war and retired in 1968 as a Wing Commander. In 2004 his account of his wartime experiences, *Lie in the Dark and Listen,* was published.

More tragedy befell the squadron en route to Malta when on 26th October one of its Wellingtons crashed near Gibraltar killing ten airmen. The remnants of 40 Squadron, comprising just six Wellingtons and a handful of crews, struggled on at Alconbury until the following February.

On 7th/8th November 1941 almost four hundred aircraft were despatched to three targets – Berlin, Cologne and Mannheim; the largest number ever

The 'nerve centre' of Bomber Command – the Operations Room at Headquarters, Naphill, High Wycombe, with Air Marshal Sir Richard Peirse and his staff in 1941.

sent out so far on a single night. Of the one hundred and sixty-nine crews sent to Berlin less than a half reached the general area of Berlin and the damage was minimal but twenty-one crews failed to return (12.4%) and over Mannheim seven were lost with no bombs recorded to have fallen on the city. In total the night's operations brought the loss of thirty-eight aircraft and almost two hundred airmen.

Such heavy losses rang serious alarm bells in Command headquarters, let alone within the War Cabinet. No force could sustain this damage for any length of time and survive. In the previous four months five hundred and twenty-six aircraft had been lost in action, probably equivalent to the Command's entire front-line strength of aircraft and crews, and perhaps not surprisingly morale in the squadrons was at an all-time low. Air Marshal Peirse claimed with some justification that the abnormal losses were largely due to an incorrect weather forecast. Nevertheless four days later he was informed that only limited operations were to be carried out in the coming months while the whole future use of Bomber Command and its strategic bombing offensive was under consideration and debate. He is reported to have said, 'It is damned hard to fight a force like Bomber Command at a subdued tone.'

For the remaining weeks of the year operations continued, but at a slow pace. In an attempt to restore confidence less well-defended targets were chosen, although on 7th/8th December Brest was once again bombed as intelligence indicated that *Scharnhorst*, *Gneisenau* and *Prinz Eugen* were soon to leave port to attack Allied shipping in the Atlantic. Brest was attacked on nine further occasions during the month; it was notorious for its heavy flak and these operations cost twenty aircraft and seventy airmen. Perhaps the most ambitious was a daylight raid, 'Veracity', on the 18th; forty-seven bombers escorted by ten fighter squadrons took part. The two Stirling squadrons each sent nine crews and suffered the heaviest casualties; both lost two aircraft, a total of thirty airmen but the Stirling gunners claimed three enemy fighters. Sir Richard Peirse sent a message to both squadrons: 'My warmest congratulations on a very successful and gallant action this afternoon.'

Perhaps the more realistic appraisal of a hard and difficult year for Bomber Command was made by Air Chief Marshal Sir Robert Saundby, K.C.B., M.C., D.F.C., in 1969; he had been Air Chief Marshal Harris's right-hand man from February 1942. He remarked: 'Throughout 1941, the Command struggled to carry out its tasks, with insufficient numbers and inadequate

Bombers over the port of Brest on 18th December – the daylight operation code-named Veracity. *(via R.H. Johnson)*

equipment...it ended a year of great effort with no increase in its strength and indeed weakened by casualties and its unsuccessful efforts to expand.'

Without question it had been a costly year with almost 1,500 aircraft lost in action and training accidents, with 3 Group bearing the heaviest loss – over four hundred and ten – of which the five Cambridgeshire squadrons lost a total of one hundred and forty-four, including fifty-five Stirlings. It is rather sad to relate that most, if not all, of the famous operations and stories of Bomber Command relate to the later years of the war, a time when the crews had the benefit of improved aircraft, sophisticated navigational aids and target marking. Nevertheless it should not be forgotten that the operations conducted during 1941 ultimately led the way to those more successful and acclaimed raids. Thus the losses sustained during this period seem to be more poignant perhaps because of the relatively small numbers of crews involved, at least when compared to the awesome might of Bomber Command in the later years.

However, the heavy bomber that proved to be the saviour of Bomber Command, the Lancaster, had made its maiden flight on 9th January 1941 and before the end of the year No 44 Squadron had received the first Lancasters to enter the Service. Additionally, two navigational aids – *Gee* and *Oboe* – had been trialled operationally. So despite the heavy losses, the disturbing Butt Report and the severe restriction on operations, there was, at least, the merest hint of a light at the end of a rather long and dark tunnel.

Chapter 5

Cometh the Hour Cometh the Man

(JANUARY-JUNE 1942)

The first six months of 1942 saw more major changes in Bomber Command than during any other period of the war; its fortunes rose dramatically from being at its lowest ebb at the end of 1941 to a force that was described as 'a potentially decisive bombing weapon'. The legendary 'Bomber' Harris arrived at the helm, the celebrated '1,000' raids were mounted, Lancasters appeared on the operational scene, the make-up of bomber crews changed, the first navigational aid was brought into action and a basic system of target marking was introduced. Thus by the end of June the Command was on the threshold of becoming a potent bombing force.

However, during January and February there were few signs of this remarkable metamorphosis. The restriction on the scale of operations remained firmly in place and January was a quiet operational month. Sir Richard Peirse's days as Commander-in-Chief were numbered, he had lost the confidence of the Air Staff, and Portal had misgivings about his judgement. On 8th January he was removed from his post and appointed the Commander of the Allied air forces in India. Sir Richard had effectively been made the scapegoat for the ills of the Command although in truth few were of his making. Jack Baldwin, No 3 Group's Commander was given temporary command until a more dynamic leader was selected, although

Portal already knew the officer he wanted – Arthur Harris; but he was in Washington leading an Air Ministry delegation and would not be available until mid-February.

The introduction of the Stirling and Halifax had resulted in another stage in the operational training programme – the conversion of crews to four-engine bombers. The first Conversion Flight (C.F.) for Stirling crews had been formed by 7 Squadron in the previous October but it quickly moved to Waterbeach, where it was first known as 26 C.F. and later 1651 Conversion Unit. Crews were expected to complete ten to twelve hours in the new bombers before being posted to an operational squadron. With this addition to operational training, it is perhaps not too surprising that Harris later maintained: 'The education of a bomber crew was the most expensive in the world: it cost some £10,000 for each man, enough to send ten men to Oxford or Cambridge for three years.'

Stirling (N6101) of 1651 Conversion Unit being loaded with sixteen 250 lb bombs – Waterbeach, 29th April 1942. In December this aircraft crashed near the runway and burnt out. (R.A.F. Museum)

Stirling crews being briefed for a 'gardening' operation.

From February onwards minelaying became an increasingly important aspect of the Command's operational schedule; code-named 'gardening', it involved the crews laying mines ('planting vegetables') from a height of 600 ft in specific locations, which were each given horticultural names such as *Nectarines* (Frisian Islands), *Artichokes* (Lorient), *Spinach* (Baltic) and *Forget-me-nots* (Kiel Canal). The Command had laid its first mines back in April 1940 but now there was an agreement with the Admiralty to lay 1,000 mines a month, providing it was not detrimental to the bombing offensive. The publication *Bomber Command* described the procedure:

> It is not unusual for the minelaying aircraft to fly around and around for a considerable time in order to make sure that the mine is laid exactly in the right place. It calls for great skill and resolution. Moreover, the crew do not have the satisfaction of even seeing the partial results of their work. There is no coloured explosion, no burgeoning of fire to report on their return home. At best all they see is a splash on the surface of a darkened and inhospitable sea.

Nevertheless, crews looked on 'gardening' as a light relief or 'easy ride' compared to operations over German targets and they considered that their chances of survival were much higher. Although from February to July 1942 eight aircraft were lost by the four Cambridgeshire squadrons, including the famous *MacRobert's Reply*, which failed to return on 17th/18th May. On one dire night, 28th/29th April 1943, no fewer than twenty-four aircraft were lost on minelaying operations near Heligoland and in the Baltic, with one hundred and fifty airmen missing in action, the heaviest 'gardening' casualties of the war. 'Gardening' has

A Stirling being loaded with mines.

received scant acknowledgement from military historians compared with other Command operations and yet it comprised 15% of its total operational sorties. A post-war analysis claimed that four hundred and ninety-one enemy vessels had been sunk and over four hundred damaged by mines dropped by the crews but at a cost of four hundred and sixty-seven aircraft; just another of the Command's contributions to the war at sea.

During January 1942, 99 Squadron lost its final and forty-third aircraft in the European war. Since September 1939 it had been in the forefront of the Command's nascent bombing offensive. The squadron now left for India where it continued as a bomber squadron. In the following month there were some other squadron changes; 101 moved its Wellington ICs to Bourn just as its crews were exchanging them for Mark IIIs. The new Mark had been provided with more powerful Bristol Hercules engines, which produced a slight increase in speed,

Wellington III of No 101 Squadron at Bourn.

and the aircraft's firepower had been improved with the addition of two .303 inch guns. On the 14th the home echelon of 40 Squadron formed the nucleus of the reformed No 156 Squadron under Wing Commander P.G.R. Heath. The squadron operated only from Cambridgeshire airfields for the whole of the war.

On the same day Bomber Command received yet another directive: 'It has been decided that the primary objective of your operations should now be focused on the morale of the enemy civil population and, in particular, of the industrial workers.' Four targets – Essen, Duisburg, Dusseldorf and Cologne – were named along with eighteen alternatives. Sir Charles Portal sought to clarify the directive, 'I suppose it is clear that the aiming points are to be the built-up areas, *not*, for instance, the dockyards or aircraft factories where these are mentioned…This must be made quite clear if it's not already understood.'

On 22nd February, the very man to prosecute such an offensive arrived at the Command's headquarters at High Wycombe as its new Air Officer Commanding – Air Marshal Arthur T. Harris – who would lead the Command for the rest of the war and whose name became synonymous with Bomber Command. Churchill is reputed to have dubbed him 'Bomber', though to his crews he was known as 'Butch'. Harris was a born leader and he quickly gained a fierce and undying loyalty from all the airmen under his command, which remained staunch throughout the war and still survives amongst the veterans of today. Although he was not responsible for the policy of area bombing, his

Air Marshal A.T. Harris with Air Vice-Marshal R.H. Saundby, his Senior Air Staff Officer.

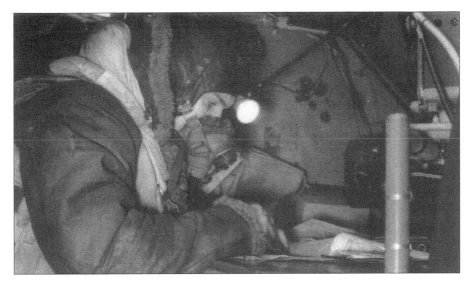

Navigator at his 'desk' in a Lancaster: the Gee *indicator at the top right.*

commitment to it was inexorable and he pursued the policy with a grim and ruthless determination. Harris famously commented: 'There are a lot of people who say that bombing cannot win the war. My reply to that is that it has never been tested...and we shall see.' A new era had begun for Bomber Command.

The *effective* strength of his Command now stood at three hundred and seventy-eight aircraft and crews, only sixty-nine being heavy bombers; well over half were the trusty Wimpys. Harris summarised its failings as 'the lack of suitable aircraft in sufficient numbers, the absence of efficient navigational aids and the deficiency of trained crews'; all these he proceeded to rectify with characteristic verve and energy. The make-up of crews was radically changed – the second pilot was dropped and a new designation of navigator was introduced, with navigation as his sole responsibility. In future the pilot would be assisted by the flight engineer. Bomb aiming was now to be performed by an air bomber or bomb aimer and the roles of air gunner and wireless operator were separated. According to the *Official History*:

> These changes had the effect of allowing each member of the crew to specialise and permitted him to receive much more thorough training...

> Without these changes Bomber Command would certainly never have approached the degree of efficiency, which it ultimately achieved.

As the Command began to mount operations night after night, the strain on bomber crews began to tell, more especially on pilots. Harris decided that a limit should be set for the number of operations flown in any tour of duty, thirty for the first and twenty for the second.

The first of several navigational aids used by crews came into operation in early March 1942 – TR1335 or *Gee*. It was a radio system that had been developed by the Telecommunications Research Establishment. The device enabled the navigator to fix a position by consulting a *Gee* box, which received two sets of pulse signals from three separate ground stations. It computed the time difference between the receipts of these signals and gave an almost instant fix. Although relatively simple and reliable to operate, it did have a range limitation of about three hundred and fifty miles but it covered targets in the Ruhr valley and some of the north-west ports. *Gee* had been first successfully trialled back in August 1941 and then large scale production of the sets began. *Gee* proved invaluable in getting crews to the target area and perhaps more importantly back to the airfield in poor weather conditions; statistics showed that after its introduction the number of aircraft landing away from the home base dropped dramatically. It was an immediate success with crews. As one navigator said, 'First impressions were of staggering accuracy, at least on practice flights in the U.K.' It was estimated that its operational life would last about six months before the enemy devised a jamming device. In fact *Gee* was first used on 8th/9th March over Essen but by May the Germans were aware of it and by August 1942 they were able to jam the system.

In order to obtain the maximum use of *Gee* with the hundred or so aircraft equipped with it, Command Headquarters developed a new bombing technique, known as *Shaker*. The main attacking force was divided into three groups – Illuminators, Target Markers and Followers. The Illuminators, all with *Gee*, would be the first over the target and would drop triple flares at ten-second intervals, with their bomb load completed with high explosives. Thus it was hoped to light the target with lines of flares approximately six miles long, which would last for maybe twelve minutes. As one airman commented, 'we struck the match for the others'. The target markers would follow, also equipped with *Gee*, carrying 'a maximum load of incendiary bombs' to provide a concentrated area of fire for the followers, without the benefit of *Gee,* arriving some fifteen minutes later with their high explosives. The *Shaker* technique was the precursor of the formation of the Pathfinder Force (PFF) later in the summer.

Harris's early tenure as Commander-in-Chief is forever remembered by the famous Lübeck operation, which along with the three '1,000 bomber' raids, demonstrated that he was the right man for the job. These memorable raids have somewhat overshadowed the bitter campaign waged against a single German city – Essen. This intense bombing offensive exemplifies the dogged and almost obsessive determination of the new Commander. The Essen raids were largely unsuccessful, which may account for the lack of notice and publicity; but they deserve greater prominence, if only for the reason of the number of airmen engaged in them – over 19,000.

Essen, a city with a population of 650,000, was situated in the Ruhr valley, which from long and bitter experience was known by crews as the 'Happy Valley' or the 'Valley of No Return'. It was considered the heartland of Germany's heavy and munitions industries and Essen, in particular, was a sprawling mass of factories dominated by the massive Krupps armaments complex right in the centre of the city and covering several hundred acres; it was first on Harris's list of Ruhr targets.

Any target in the Ruhr was difficult and dangerous as they were heavily defended by anti-aircraft and searchlight batteries. One crewman famously described the flak as so heavy that 'you could get out and walk on it'! The route from the Dutch coast, some 150 miles, was fraught with night fighters. Even when the crews arrived over the Ruhr an almost permanent industrial haze, even on moonlit nights, made accurate bombing almost impossible. The Air Staff considered Essen 'the supreme target', but it was more heavily defended than any other Ruhr target, known to the crews as 'Flak City' and thought to be on a par with Berlin as the heaviest defended German target.

Since November 1940 Essen had been attacked nine times at a cost of thirty-two aircraft and over one hundred and ten airmen but without any serious damage being inflicted. From 8th/9th March until 16th/17th June 1942 thirteen raids were mounted to this 'supreme target' but sadly there was minimal damage either to the city or the Krupps factories. Each successive operation was noted as 'not successful' or 'disappointing results'. With some reluctance Air Marshal Harris abandoned the campaign, or at least put it on hold for three months. It had been a rather costly experience both in men and machines; over one hundred and seventy aircraft and eight hundred and ninety-five airmen were lost in action. The majority of these airmen are

Reichswald Forest War Cemetery near Kleve contains the graves of 3,971 airmen.
(via B. Jones)

buried in Reichswald Forest War Cemetery, near Kleve, which contains the largest number of airmen (3,971) of any German war cemetery.

On 1st March 1942 a new airfield opened at Graveley, four miles south of Huntingdon, and it was intended to operate as a satellite for nearby Tempsford. No 161 (Special Duties) Squadron arrived from Stradishall where it had been engaged in dropping agents and supplies to support the Resistance fighters in the occupied countries. Only three clandestine operations were mounted from the airfield before the squadron moved to Tempsford. Graveley did not become fully operational until August when it housed one of the original Pathfinder squadrons.

The first major success against a German target came with the raid on Lübeck on 28th/29th March. The old Hanseatic port on the Baltic Sea was thought to be relatively lightly defended and the narrow streets and timbered buildings in the *Alstradt* (old town) made it 'a particularly suitable target for testing the effect of a very heavy attack with incendiary bombs'. Although it was beyond the range of *Gee*, one hundred and ninety-one out of the two hundred and thirty-four crews claimed to have bombed the target. In two hours over 400 tons of bombs were dropped, two-thirds of them incendiaries, and 60% of the buildings were destroyed, mainly by fire. It was a virtually perfect example of area bombing with the Command claiming that one hundred and ninety acres had been flattened, the first time acreage had been used in a post-raid analysis to quantify bomb damage.

The success of the raid provided a boost to the Command's morale and was greeted with great acclaim by the British public, who were sorely in need of some evidence that the country was hitting back at Germany. Harris later recalled, 'on the night of 28th/29th March, the first German city went up in flames'. Thirteen aircraft were lost (5.1%) and three were from the ten Stirlings despatched by 7 Squadron; twenty-one airmen were killed including Captain J. F. Wyn-Griffith, Royal Artillery, one of a number of Army officers drafted into the R.A.F. as air gunners. The Lübeck raid was a portent for the German people of all the horrors of heavy bombing that were to come in the months ahead. The raid so incensed the German High Command that Hitler personally ordered retaliation raids on similar English cities, 'any listed in *Baedeker*' – hence the raids during April and May on Exeter, Norwich, Canterbury, and Bath.

Towards the end of April it was the turn of another Baltic port – Rostock – to suffer four raids over five nights. There were many similarities with the earlier Lubeck raid, a concentrated area bombing of a lightly defended town, but also with separate precision attacks on a large Heinkel aircraft factory

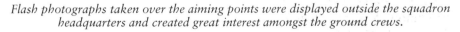

Flash photographs taken over the aiming points were displayed outside the squadron headquarters and created great interest amongst the ground crews.

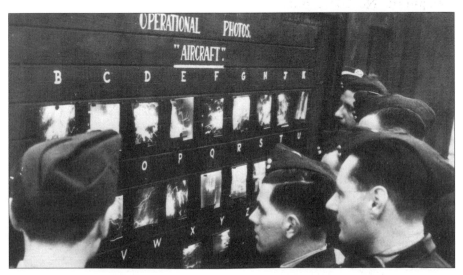

on the southern outskirts. The first raid took place on the 23rd/24th and it was not really until the fourth raid, on 26th/27th April, that the greatest damage was done. The Command claimed that 130 acres or 60% of the town centre had been destroyed. The *Official History* called this final raid a 'masterpiece...a resounding success', and moreover the losses were minimal at eight aircraft (1.5%). For the first time the German High Command described a raid as *Terrorangriff* ('terror raid') and it was recorded that 'community life in Rostock is practically at an end'.

During May 1942, Harris conceived a plan that was not only bold and audacious in the extreme but also most ambitious in the light of the operational strength of his Command at the time, little more than four hundred bombers. He proposed to send a force of 1,000 bombers to a German city on a single night. Hitherto the highest number had been two hundred and seventy-two to Hamburg on 8th/9th April. His plan, code-named 'Millennium', received the approval of the Air Staff and more especially Winston

Wellington crew prepare for an operation – fleece-lined jackets, flying rations, thermos of coffee or soup and a parachute.

Churchill, who was prepared to accept the loss of one hundred aircraft.

To achieve the magical figure Harris sought the help of Coastal Command and Flying Training Command, but subsequently the Admiralty refused to allow Coastal Command to take part and the bombers offered by Flying Training were considered ill-equipped for night bombing. So Harris had little alternative than to use training crews at O.T.U.s and Conversion Units, which ultimately supplied three hundred and sixty-five, mostly flown by instructors and screened pilots. This was a brave and potentially dangerous decision to make because if the training crews suffered heavy losses it would have a paralysing effect on the planned expansion of the Command.

Command Headquarters introduced the concept of a bomber stream, in which all the aircraft would fly a common route, at the same speed to and from the target and with each aircraft being allotted a specific height band and time slot to lessen the risk of collision. It was also decided to reduce the time for actual bombing to ninety minutes, a revolutionary decision. By 26th May all the plans were in place with Hamburg as the target; everything now depended on a favourable weather forecast for the end of the month as the full moon period approached. But for three days the weather over Germany was not suitable for such a massive operation and on 30th May Harris decided to change the target to his second choice, Cologne. Shortly after noon the message went out to the fifty-three airfields engaged in the operation to attack Cologne that night.

The briefing for the operation took place at 6 pm at each airfield and when the crews were told that it was Cologne, there was considerable relief that it was not going to be Berlin. When they were informed that they were going to just one target with more than 1,000 aircraft taking part the reaction was quite amazing, cheering broke out and this had to be silenced for Harris's message to them to be read out:

> The force of which you form a part tonight is at least twice the size and has more than four times the carrying capacity of the largest air force ever before concentrated on one objective. You have the opportunity therefore, to strike a blow at the enemy which will resound, not only through Germany, but throughout the world...Press home your attack with the utmost determination and resolution in the foreknowledge that if you succeed, the most shattering and devastating blow will have been delivered against the very vitals of the enemy. Let him have it – right on the chin.

Neumarkt, the centre of Cologne, one week after the Millenium operation, the Cathedral still standing to the left of the railway station.

On this momentous night 1,047 aircraft left with 3 Group supplying the largest number – two hundred and twenty-two – and the doughty Wellingtons at six hundred and two greatly outnumbering the rest of the force. The first fifteen minutes of the attack would be made by *Gee*-equipped aircraft with two Stirlings of XV Squadron leading the force; they were flown by Wing Commander J.C. Macdonald, D.F.C., A.F.C., and Squadron Leader R.S. Gilmore. They left Wyton at 22.30 hours and at forty-seven minutes past midnight the first bombs were dropped on the *Neumarkt*, the centre of the old town. In just ninety minutes eight hundred and ninety-eight crews dropped over 1,450 tons of bombs, two-thirds of them incendiaries, and returning crews reported that they could see the fires from a distance of some one hundred and forty miles.

Forty-one aircraft (3.9%) were lost, which was the highest on a single raid, and remarkably the losses of training crews were less than the regular crews. However, 26 O.T.U., which was based in Wing but had used Graveley as an advanced base, lost four crews. Despite the deep concern about collisions there were only two, precisely the figure estimated by the Command's 'boffins'. All but two of the Cambridgeshire squadrons escaped without casualties. No 156 lost two aircraft – eleven airmen killed – and the squadron were still coming to terms with the loss of their Commander, Wing

Commander P.G.R. Heath, killed on the previous night; 101 Squadron also lost two aircraft, one of which suffered engine trouble on the way out, when the five airmen baled out and were taken prisoner. The pilot, Pilot Officer Reece Read, well remembered the steady and ceaseless drone of aircraft passing overhead as he lay helpless on the ground. Read, a twenty-eight year old, was on his eighth operation; before the war he had been a mining engineer in West Africa but had returned to volunteer for flying duties. He had always wanted to be a doctor so he used his time as a prisoner of war to study medicine.

Another pilot taken prisoner on the night, Flight Sergeant John H. Bulford, also used his time in captivity to study, in his instance – economics. He was the captain of one of 11 O.T.U.'s Wellingtons. Although he was only twenty years old when he arrived at Bassingbourn to serve as an instructor, he was already a hardened veteran and was very young to reach the rank of Flight Sergeant. Bulford's Wellington IC, which was rather aged, also suffered engine problems on the return flight from Cologne. Perhaps it can be said that being captured was the final salvation for crews in damaged aircraft but most never viewed it as such; they saw it in far simpler terms – you went out on an operation and either you returned or you 'got the chop'. By the time any news of capture filtered back to the squadron, most of the personnel had changed and few faces or names were remembered.

The Cologne raid was a complete and utter success, which dealt a shattering blow to the German High Command; newspapers hailed it as the 'World's Biggest Air Raid' and claimed that it was the first 'victory' of the war. The general public heaped praise upon the Command and its 'heroic airmen', while Harris became a well-known celebrity and was knighted on 4th June. The raid was an important turning point for Bomber Command and confirmed its arrival as a major bombing force. It also established Harris as a fine and inspirational leader; John Terraine in *The Right of the Line* commented, '[his] calm and deliberate decision to stake the whole of his force and its future on that night, showed the true quality of command'.

Harris was keen to maintain the momentum and replicated the '1,000 raid' on 1st/2nd June with, needless to say, Essen as the target. Only (!) nine hundred and fifty-six aircraft were available for this operation but once again the heavy industrial haze and a layer of low cloud saved the city and the bombing was very scattered with several nearby towns – Oberhausen, Duisburg and Mulheim – suffering heavy damage. One of No 7's Stirlings was lost just off the Dutch coast. It was piloted by Flight Lieutenant N. E.

Stirling III (W7513) 'LS-R' of XV Squadron at Wyton on 2nd June 1942 after returning from Essen. The aircraft later went to No 75 (NZ) Squadron and went missing on 28th/29th June 1943 whilst on a 'gardening' operation; the seven airmen were killed. (via J. Adams)

Fitch, who was on his second operational tour; also on board was Group Captain Herbert M. Massey, D.S.O., M.C., a Royal Flying Corps veteran, who had volunteered for service and was acting as Second Pilot ('Second Dickey' in R.A.F. slang). All the crew survived as prisoners of war and Massey became the Senior British Officer at *Stalag-Luft* III, Sagan and was there at the time of the famous 'Great Escape'. It has since been calculated that 4th June 1942 was the mid-point of the war and it is sobering to reflect that three-quarters of the Command's total casualties were yet to come.

One of the eight hundred and sixty-five airmen lost in action during these costly and largely ineffectual Essen raids was Sergeant Guy H. Chamberlin. Although the death of each individual airman of Bomber Command was tragic, certainly to their family, friends and colleagues, the circumstances and manner of his death may be considered even more so. And yet like thousands upon thousands of Bomber Command airmen, his name is now just another statistic in the long and grim catalogue of losses suffered by the Command during the Second World War.

In many respects Guy Chamberlin could be considered an epitome of the airmen who served in the Command in the early war years. He had entered the R.A.F. in May 1940 and was recommended for flying duties at the age of thirty, albeit rather old compared with other volunteers; indeed the recruiting posters for pilots required men 'from 17¼ and not yet 31'. However, Guy already held a private pilot's licence and was selected for pilot training, finally receiving his coveted 'wings' in October 1941. One month later he was posted to No 20 O.T.U. at Lossiemouth where he trained on Wellingtons. On 1st May 1942 he was posted to 156 Squadron, then operating Wellington IIIs which were equipped with *Gee* and whose crews acted as target markers in an embryonic 'pathfinder' role. Seven days later he was sent on his first operation, over eleven months since he had started his flying training, such was the length of time required to train a bomber pilot.

Sergeant Guy H. Chamberlin of No 156 Squadron. (Courtesy David Chamberlin)

On 5th/6th June, Essen was the target for the eleventh time in three months and Sergeant Chamberlin was one of the seventy-eight airmen from 156 Squadron detailed for the operation. His original crew had been lost in a training accident in Scotland, whilst he had been on sick leave, so on this night he joined another crew as Second Pilot to Pilot Officer E.A. Smith, R.C.A.F.: he and his crew were making their twenty-ninth operation whereas it was Guy's fourth. It is not known whether the crew had already marked the target and were on their way home, but over Geldern, a small town to the north-west of Essen and near the Dutch border, their Wellington was struck probably by the starboard wing of a Wellington IC of No 103 Squadron. The two aircraft crashed to the ground, nine airmen were killed and the only survivor of this tragic accident was the pilot of 103's Wellington – Flight Lieutenant Walter Morison. Sergeant Chamberlin and the other eight airmen are now buried in Reichswald Forest War Cemetery. No 156 lost another crew on this night, shot down by a night fighter over Holland.

Many crews had a psychological fear of collisions, although in truth those between 'friendly' aircraft were quite rare considering the increasing number of aircraft involved in operations, a far greater risk was the collision with enemy night fighters. Indeed on the same night a Stirling of 149 Squadron collided with a Messerschmitt 110 and ditched in the North Sea; all but one of the crew was rescued. As all Bomber Command veterans will admit, however experienced or well-drilled a crew might be, luck played a significant part in deciding those who lived and those who died. On this night Guy Chamberlin's luck had sadly deserted him, as it had for his fellow airmen; especially distressing considering that they needed just one more sortie to complete their operational tour.

This unfortunate collision was one of those remarkable and strange coincidences thrown up by the war; Flight Lieutenant Morison had been Guy Chamberlin's flying instructor at 20 O.T.U.! Walter Morison survived as a prisoner of war and has related his wartime experiences in *Flak and Ferrets: One way to Colditz*. When later asked what he did in the war, he replied:

> Not a lot. Learnt to fly. Taught some people to fly. Dropped some bombs. Taken prisoner. Escaped. Tried to borrow an aircraft from the Luftwaffe. Caught. Sent to Colditz. That was all there was really. A very ordinary war.

Such is the quiet and unassuming modesty shown by all the veterans that were fortunate enough to survive; their normal response is, 'I did nothing special, I just did my duty'!

The third and final '1,000 raid' was mounted on 25th/26th June 1942 to Bremen. The Command was at first unable to reach the symbolic figure, falling thirty short despite using all the valuable resources of the Training and Conversion units. But the force did include every single type of bomber – heavy, medium and light – then in operation with the Command; this was for the first and only occasion. However, Churchill intervened and the Admiralty were forced to provide over one hundred bombers, so the final total of 1,067 exceeded that of the Cologne raid. A large Focke-Wulf aircraft factory and two U-boat yards were separately targeted. The results of this raid were not as dramatic as Cologne but certainly it was an improvement on the Essen operation and the time over the target had been reduced to sixty-five minutes. In total fifty-five aircraft were lost (4.9%) but sadly the training crews suffered far higher losses – thirty-four. That Air Marshal

H.M. King George VI at Waterbeach on 12th June 1942. Flight Lieutenant Peter Boggis, D.F.C., is shaking hands with the King, Air Marshal J. Baldwin, A.O.C. of No 3 Group, is on the far left. (R.A.F. Museum)

Harris was not happy with this operation is clear from his decision to return to Bremen on the nights of the 27th/28th and the 29th/30th, which resulted in the loss of another fifteen crews, but the raids were only considered 'moderate successes'.

In the mere four months since Harris's arrival, Bomber Command had made a remarkable recovery, clearly demonstrating that it was capable of inflicting heavy damage on German cities and towns. As Churchill declared, after the Cologne raid: 'this is proof of the growing power of the British bomber force and is the herald of what Germany will receive, city by city, from now on'. Such an exceptional change of fortunes had been achieved at a considerable cost – six hundred and twelve aircraft or 4.25%. Although this was slightly below the 'tolerable' rate, the crews had about a 45% chance of surviving one tour and less than 20% chance of achieving two tours. Since 23rd February over 3,500 airmen had gone missing in action, of which number six hundred and fifty survived as prisoners of war. These airmen can be considered the first 'pathfinders'; they lost their lives whilst proving the bombing procedures and techniques which, with certain modifications, would become the standard practice in the years ahead.

Chapter 6

Enter the Pathfinders

(JULY-DECEMBER 1942)

Air Marshal Sir Arthur Harris had already made his mark on Bomber Command and during July there would be no relief for his crews as he continued an almost ceaseless and relentless bombardment of German targets. Nevertheless, he was well aware of how much he relied on the courage and determination of his crews. Indeed, on 4th July 1942, in a letter to Winston Churchill he vividly captured the nightly ordeal of these brave airmen:

> ...the 2 o'clock in the morning courage of lonely men, their actions hidden by darkness from their fellows, determined to press home their attacks through fantastically violent defence barrages into the searchlight cones, wherein gunfire concentrates immediately on any aircraft illuminated. Their behaviour cannot be watched, it can seldom even be judged by an individual. Only after the event and by results achieved do we ever know how went the fight. We seldom know, except by implication, which crews made the greatest contribution. You would be the first to appreciate how dependent we are on the high courage and qualities of the leaders.

During four nights in July a total of 1,013 aircraft bombed Duisburg, Germany's largest inland port, and Hamburg. For the first of these Hamburg

A Halifax crew is cheered as they prepare to take off.

raids on the 26th/27th, Harris called for 'a full maximum effort', which then amounted to some four hundred aircraft and crews; in fact four hundred and three were sent and twenty-one lost (7.2%). The crews had to contend with heavy cloud and icing on the journey out but there were clear skies over the target and Command Headquarters recorded that 'severe and widespread damage' had been inflicted.

Nevertheless the following night another large operation, 'Derby', was mounted to Hamburg but bad weather over the airfields in northern England resulted in only No 3 Group and training crews from 91 Group actually taking part. As the weather worsened the training crews were recalled and it turned out to be a dire night for the Group; only sixty-eight crews claimed to have bombed out of one hundred and sixty-five and the losses were catastrophic – sixteen Wellingtons and nine Stirlings (over 15%). Three Wellingtons of 156 Squadron failed to return and the seventeen airmen missing in action included Wing Commander H.L. Price, D.F.C., who had commanded the squadron for barely three months.

Two nights later over one hundred training crews joined the main force bombing Düsseldorf; six hundred and thirty aircraft were engaged and for the first time more than one hundred Lancasters were sent out. Twenty-nine crews were lost but of these eleven came from training units and a number of 'screened pilots' were lost. Serving as an instructor at an O.T.U. during this time must have felt little different from their days on an operational squadron!

By contrast the first two weeks of August were quiet, although on two successive nights – the 11th to 13th – Mainz, one of Germany's oldest cities and situated on the Rhine, was bombed; it was believed to be lightly defended and eleven crews were lost in the two raids but three came from 156 Squadron and two from XV Squadron. During this relatively peaceful period it was almost as if Command Headquarters was waiting patiently for the arrival of the Pathfinder Force.

Although Bomber Command had early on recognised the importance of

'Everything stops for tea' – Lancaster crews enjoy a 'cuppa' before an air test.

radio-navigational aids, the concept of a 'Target Finding Force' was not actively explored until late 1941. The main proponent was Group Captain S. 'Syd' O. Bufton, D.S.O., D.F.C., who had recently been appointed Deputy Director of Bomber Operations at the Air Ministry. He had operational experience with No 4 Group, where he had pioneered various projects aimed at helping the 'best' crews to locate targets using flares and coloured lights. His paper, which he presented in March, envisaged six squadrons 'based in close proximity' manned by normal crews but including 'at least 40 experienced crews of high navigational abilities'. Faced with the disturbing Butt Report, Bufton was able to convince his fellow staff officers of the need for such a force, but to persuade the A.O.C. of Bomber Command and his Group Commanders was quite another matter.

The Pathfinder Force's Badge – 'We Guide to Strike'.

Soon after Harris arrived at Bomber Command he was approached on the subject, but he was firmly opposed to the proposal. He felt that the formation of a *corps d'élite* would siphon off the best crews, be detrimental to squadron morale and could also jeopardise the crews' chances of promotion. He favoured a system of 'raid leaders', with one selected squadron operating in each Group. He was aware that *Gee* would soon be universally available and this he felt would bring about improved performance. After endless debate and correspondence Sir Charles Portal, who strongly supported Bufton's proposals, overruled Harris and, in June, a 'Target Finding Force' was approved.

Despite his initial opposition Harris now took up the project with his usual verve and energy and he managed to accomplish some important changes to the format of the new Force. He instructed the Commanders of his four heavy bomber Groups to nominate a squadron to form the Force, rather than transferring their best crews. The original name did not appeal to him, so instead he proposed the 'Pathfinder Force' (PFF), which he felt implied 'a navigational aid'. To compensate for the possible loss of promotion and for the fact that the crews would be required to complete a tour of forty-five operations, he persuaded the Air Ministry, and more especially the Treasury, that crews seconded to the Pathfinders would be accorded one rank higher than they held. Finally and quite surprisingly considering his views on elitism, he gained approval, by Royal warrant, for the Force's own special badge – the famous gilt hovering eagle – to be worn

on the flap of the left-hand breast pocket below the medal ribbons when the airman had qualified as a 'Path Finder', usually after ten PFF sorties. It was made clear that the badge should not be worn whilst on operations!

The Pathfinder Force came into being on 15th August 1942 under the command of Group Captain Donald C. T. Bennett, D.S.O. He was a relatively young Australian pilot with a distinguished pre-war flying record, both with the R.A.F. and Imperial Airways, and he

Air Vice-Marshal Donald Bennett, C.B., C.B.E., D.S.O., wearing his Pathfinder Badge.

Lancaster I 'OL-Y' of No 83 Squadron.

was acknowledged as the Service's leading navigational expert. Bennett had commanded a Halifax squadron in 4 Group and had only recently returned from Sweden after making his escape when shot down over Norway. It was a truly inspirational choice, and much of the Pathfinders' later success was due to his strong leadership, vision, drive and great determination. Harris later described him as 'the most efficient airman I have ever met. His courage, both moral and physical, is outstanding, and as a technician he is unrivalled.' The Group's badge was not finally authorised until March 1955. The eight-point star not only suggested the number of the Group but also symbolised astro-navigation and the flaming arrow represented the target markers dropped by its aircraft, with the motto '*We Guide To Strike*'.

Bennett established his headquarters at Wyton with his four squadrons close at hand. The new Force was nominally under the control of 3 Group but Bennett reported directly to Command Headquarters. On 17th August the PFF was effectively in place; 156 Squadron moved from Alconbury to Warboys, 7 Squadron was moved out of 3 Group into the PFF but still remained at Oakington, 35 Squadron with its Halifax IIs moved down from Leeming to the new station at Graveley and the Lancasters of 83 Squadron from Scampton were based at Wyton, which meant that XV Squadron moved out to Bourn.

The PFF squadrons were thrown into the battle with high hopes of success but with few, if any, advantages. The crews held no more special skills than other crews and there was no new equipment or indeed devices for marking targets. They also began their difficult and dangerous role when the German defences had been greatly strengthened and the enemy had now discovered the means to jam *Gee*. It would be difficult to conceive of a more hazardous time to test the mettle of the pioneer Pathfinders, especially as Harris readily acknowledged that 'we shall ask indeed much of them'. Although the crews of the first four squadrons had no choice in the matter, subsequent replacement PFF crews would all be volunteers, having already volunteered for flying duties.

The formation of the PFF brought three new aircraft to the Cambridgeshire skies – the Handley Page Halifax, Avro Lancaster and de Havilland Mosquito.

The Halifax owed its existence to an Air Ministry specification (P13/36) for a twin-engine bomber powered by the new Rolls-Royce Vulture engines, although it was later designed to take four Rolls-Royce Merlin engines. The first prototype (L7244) flew on 25th October 1939 and about twelve months later it entered the Service with 35 Squadron at Leeming, commencing operations on 10th/11th March 1941. The Mark II cruised about 190 mph with a total bomb load of 13,000 lbs and a ceiling height of 22,000 ft. It was armed with eight .303 Brownings in nose, mid-upper and tail turrets. The aircraft proved to be most durable and inspired a strong loyalty among its crews, who fondly called it the 'Halibag'! Air Marshal Harris was not particularly enamoured with it and he made no secret of the fact that he would have willingly traded them for more Lancasters. During March to August 1942 the aircraft suffered more heavily than the Lancasters and the losses were considered sufficiently serious (10% in August) to rest the Halifax squadrons for about a month. Nevertheless the Halifax served with distinction in three Commands undertaking a variety of roles. The greatly improved Mark IIIs, which came into service in October 1943, fully restored the aircraft's reputation and over 6,370 Halifaxes were produced.

What can one say about the quite remarkable Lancaster, which really epitomised Bomber Command during the last three years of the war? It had come into being almost by accident when its predecessor, the twin-engine Manchester failed to live up to expectations. The prototype Avro 683 flew on 9th January 1941 powered by four Merlin X engines and it entered the Service in the following December. On 10th/11th March 1942 just two Lancasters were engaged in the Essen raid. The Mark Is had a maximum speed of about 285 mph and cruised at 210 mph. It was originally designed to carry 4,000 lbs of bombs but this figure steadily rose up to the 12,000 lb (*Tallboy*) bomb and ultimately the massive 22,000 lb (*Grand Slam*) bomb; it was the only Allied bomber capable of carrying these bombs. The Lancaster had three gun turrets – nose, dorsal and tail – and over 7,370 were built with Mark Is and III accounting for over 87% of the production.

The Mosquito was, without a shadow of doubt, the most successful and versatile Allied aircraft of the Second World War. It operated with equal facility as a low-level and high-altitude bomber, a day and night fighter, or an anti-shipping strike aircraft and was ideal for photo-reconnaissance; but its greatest successes were gained in the Pathfinder Force with the use of *Oboe* and in the legendary Light Night Striking Force. The Mosquito I was provided with two Rolls-Royce Merlin engines and when it entered the Service in July 1941 it proved to be faster than the current Spitfire. The first bomber variant, BIV, entered Bomber Command in November 1941 with 105 Squadron but it was not until the end of the following May that the Mosquito bomber made its operational debut. By the end of the war well over 39,000 Mosquito sorties had been flown by the Command for the loss of two hundred and sixty aircraft – a quite remarkable casualty rate of 0.65%!

On the very day (17th August 1942) that the embryonic PFF was in place and ready for action, twelve B-17s of the U.S.A.A.F. Eighth Air Force made a bombing attack on railway yards at Rouen. Bomber Command now had a daylight partner in the strategic bombing offensive. Soon German targets would be bombed both by day and night and Cambridgeshire could claim to be 'bomber country'. In September, Alconbury was handed over to the U.S.A.A.F., followed in October by Bassingbourn; the new airfields at Molesworth, Kimbolton, Little Staughton and Glatton were also allocated to the U.S.A.A.F. The day also proved momentous for Bomber Command when a solitary crew made the last operational Blenheim sortie in the Command; in the weeks ahead two other celebrated bombers – Whitley and Hampden – were removed from bombing operations. What with the arrival of the Pathfinder Force, certainly 'times were a-changing'.

The first PFF operation was mounted against Flensburg on 18th/19th August and although sixteen of the thirty-one PFF crews claimed to have marked the target, the bombing was less than impressive. Flight Lieutenant G.P. Greenup and his crew of 156 Squadron were the first Pathfinders to cross the German coast and reach the target. His report demonstrates the problems faced by the crews:

> Flares only carried. Target not definitely identified. Searched for 15 minutes and unable to pinpoint due to haze and bad visibility. Did not drop flares in case mainforce be misled thereby. 17 bundles of flares brought back.

The Force lost their first aircraft and crew in action – a Halifax of 35 Squadron. Six nights later (the 24th/25th) the operation to Frankfurt was not too successful and five PFF crews were lost. Although Kassel was heavily

---

Halifax II (W7676) 'TL-P' of 35 Squadron, shot down on 28th/29th August 1942 – all seven crewmen were killed.

bombed on the 27th/28th there was little cloud over the target area so that the PFF crews were able to visually illuminate the target. Flight Lieutenant N. Gilmour, D.F.C., of 156 Squadron was reported to have made 'a very fine show in marking the target'.

The following night Nuremberg was the target; this city was of great significance to the Nazi party, it was where the infamous pre-war Nazi rallies were held. Rudimentary target marking bombs were used for the first time – 250 lb bomb casings filled with inflammable material and chemicals called 'Red Blob Flares'; they were dropped with great accuracy. It was considered a successful operation with 'considerable scattered damage throughout the city'. Sadly it was a costly operation with twenty-three of one hundred and fifty-three aircraft lost (14%) including six PFF aircraft. The Wellingtons' crews suffered harshly, fourteen out of forty-one failing to return (34%). Flight Lieutenant Gilmour's Wellington III was lost on this operation; he was on his forty-seventh operation, and also in his crew was another 'veteran' airman, Flight Lieutenant A. C. Spenser, D.F.M., who had previously served with 101 Squadron. The steady loss of such experienced and valuable airmen over the months ahead would be a concern for Group Captain Bennett and his staff.

On 1st/2nd September 1942 when Saarbrücken was the target, Saarlouis, a town thirteen miles to the north-west, was marked and bombed in error. The PFF had its critics within the Service and soon the news went round that the Pathfinders had 'put up a black' – R.A.F. slang for a duty or task done badly. However, the following night over Karlsruhe eighteen PFF crews marked the target very accurately and 'very heavy damage' was inflicted, some '260 acres devastated'.

The operation to Bremen on 4th/5th September heralded the introduction of a new PFF procedure. The Force was divided into *Illuminators*, leading crews with white flares, *Primary Visual Markers* with coloured flares and *Backers-Up* with incendiaries to drop on the coloured flares. This basic pattern would form the standard procedure of future PFF operations with the introduction of special target-indicator bombs. It proved to be a most successful raid. Düsseldorf was the target on the 10th/11th when *Pink Pansies* were used for the first time; they were 4,000 lb bomb casings stuffed with benzol, rubber and phosphorous, which exploded in a great pink flash. It was a successful operation with very heavy damage sustained and 'at least 120 acres devastated', although at a high cost with thirty-three out of four hundred and seventy-nine aircraft lost – 6.8%.

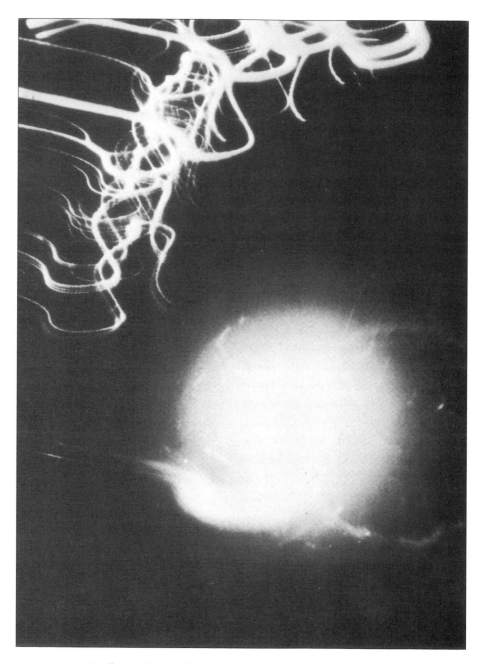

A 4,000 lb 'Cookie' explodes on Karlsruhe, 2nd/3rd September 1942.

Six nights later (the 16th/17th) the Command suffered heavier losses when thirty-nine aircraft (10.6%) went missing over that most difficult and dangerous target – Essen. There was at least some consolation that it was considered the most successful raid to date. Nineteen training crews failed to return, including three from 11 O.T.U. at Steeple Morden. After this Essen raid no further trainee crews were sent on bombing operations, their live 'operational experience' being confined to 'Nickel' operations over enemy occupied countries.

The sheer determination and calm resolve of the Command's pilots and crewmen can best be illustrated by several incidents during this period. On 10th/11th September whilst engaged on the Düsseldorf raid a Stirling, *T-Tommy*, of 7 Squadron piloted by Flying Officer J. P. Trench was coned by searchlights over Maastricht on the return flight. The aircraft was hit by flak, which severely damaged the port engines, one of which 'left the bulkhead'. After jettisoning all moveable objects and ammunition casings the Stirling struggled across the North Sea and the English coast at a height of barely 150 ft. It finally crash-landed at Weeley, Essex. Some of the crew were able to make their escape before a fire started but they went back into the aircraft to rescue other members before the aircraft exploded. The rear gunner, Pilot Officer W.N. Gledding, was blown out by the explosion. The front gunner and flight engineer were killed. Flying Officer Trench was later awarded the D.S.O., the navigator, Pilot Officer O.L. Selman the D.F.C. and the wireless operator, Sergeant I. J. Edwards, the D.F.M.; the tragic incident was officially recorded as 'an outstanding example of courage and determination on the part of the captain and the crew'.

The Distinguished Service Order had been established in 1886 for 'meritorious or distinguished service in the field or before the enemy', being second only to the Victoria Cross. During the Second World War no less than eight hundred and seventy were awarded to R.A.F. airmen. The Distinguished Flying Cross, instituted in 1918, was to recognise acts of 'valour, courage or devotion to duty whilst flying in active operations against the enemy' by officers, with the Distinguished Flying Medal for N.C.O. airmen. Many of these medals were awarded 'immediately' for specific acts of bravery, although the majority were granted at the end of an operational tour. Over 19,000 D.F.C.s and some 6,630 D.F.M.s were awarded. Each of these three medals had added 'Bars' to recognise subsequent acts of bravery. In the light of these awards to the three PFF airmen, it is interesting to note that Air Marshal Harris wrote to Group Captain Bennett in November to ensure that any member of the PFF received just reward if he managed to complete his extended tour of operations:

> I am always against any sort of automatic award. Nevertheless I want you to see to it that no member of any Pathfinder crew who completes the full 45 sorties fails to get an award, unless for some special reason you consider he has not earned one.

On 19th/20th September a remarkable escape was made by a New Zealand pilot, Squadron Leader A. 'Artie' or 'Pedro' Ashworth, D.F.C., A.F.C., of 156 Squadron. His crew was returning from Saarbrücken when some flares ignited in the aircraft; they were highly volatile and Ashworth ordered the crew to bale out. He could not locate his parachute but by some adroit flying he managed to extinguish the fires and successfully brought his Wellington III back single-handed to land at West Malling. Ashworth had previously served with the celebrated 75 (New Zealand) Squadron. In 1943 he moved to the PFF Headquarters; whilst he was there the code-name

Distinguished Flying Cross and Distinguished Flying Medal. (Spink & Son Ltd.)

Waganui was introduced for 'sky markers' (parachute flares); this was his home town in New Zealand. Ashworth later returned to operational flying with No 635 Squadron, when it joined the PFF in 1944.

Although it might be considered somewhat invidious to pick out just a few airmen from the many that served in the early days of the Pathfinders, the loss of Wing Commander J. 'Jimmie' H. Marks, D.S.O., D.F.C., Commander of 35 Squadron, on the same Saarbrücken operation was a serious blow not only to the PFF but to the Service as a whole. Marks was a pre-war regular officer, who had long experience as a bomber pilot. Back in June 1940 flying Whitleys with 77 Squadron, he had some ideas about the use of 'pathfinding' techniques and also using the squadron's four best navigators to head a raid. When he was appointed to command 35 Squadron in March 1942 he was only twenty years old, the youngest Wing Commander in the Service. As one of his crew later recalled, he was 'a brilliant pilot, a wonderful leader and a man this country could not afford to lose'.

Wing Commander J. 'Jimmie' H. Marks, D.S.O., D.F.C., Commander of No 35 Squadron. (R.A.F. Museum)

Just two weeks later another of 156's pilots, Flight Lieutenant Greenup, repeated Ashworth's feat when, on 5th October, his Wellington III was struck by lightning whilst crossing the French coast bound for Aachen. The flares were jettisoned and the aircraft was subjected to heavy flak, so much so that the crew baled out but Greenup managed to coax the heavily damaged bomber back and make a crash-landing at Manston.

Whilst the PFF was gaining valuable experience the only other operational squadron in Cambridgeshire, No XV at Bourn, was also engaged in bombing the same targets. They lost twenty Stirlings in action compared with No 7, which lost twenty-one Stirlings over the same period. Although XV did lose another aircraft in training and two during air tests; one which crashed on 29th October resulted in eleven fatalities including a 'sky pilot' – RAF slang for a padre; Squadron Leader C.G. Fisher, the Station Padre, had merely gone on this flight to gain air experience!

In the late autumn Bomber Command was diverted to bomb the industrial cities of northern Italy to support the Eighth Army's imminent offensive at El Alamein and Operation Torch, the Allied invasion of north-west Africa. There were six night raids on the port of Genoa, seven to Turin where the large Fiat motor works was the prime target and one daylight raid on Milan, which had a dire effect on Italian morale. Despite the distance (about 1,400 miles), the long flying time (ten hours or maybe longer) and having to negotiate the Alps, these Italian operations were quite favoured by the crews as the Italian flak was certainly far lighter and less accurate than that experienced over German targets. In fact almost 1,800 sorties were flown for the loss of twenty-seven aircraft in action – a mere 2.0%. However, these operations did result in some remarkable feats of heroism, courage and determination.

On 18th/19th November 1942 perhaps the most exceptional 'solo' flight was accomplished by a Halifax pilot – Squadron Leader Basil V. Robinson, D.S.O., D.F.C., A.F.C., of 35 Squadron. Whilst bound for Turin one of the flares in the bomb bay ignited and the fire quickly spread to the port wing. The crew were ordered to bale out and just as Robinson was preparing to make his escape, he realised that the fire had gone out. Robinson returned to the controls and managed to bring the Halifax home – over seven hundred miles and some four hours flying time. He finally landed safely at Colerne in Wiltshire and for this epic flight he was awarded a Bar to his D.S.O. – a very rare occurrence. Back in December 1941 Robinson had had another lucky escape when his Halifax ditched in the sea about sixty miles off the English coast; the aircraft floated for about twenty minutes enabling the crew to be rescued. Sadly, Robinson pressed his luck too far. He was killed in action over Berlin on 23rd/24th August 1943 when he was a Group Captain and Station Commander of Graveley and as such there was no obligation on him to take part in the operation.

Two nights later (20th/21st) when Turin was again the target, one of XV Squadron's Stirlings piloted by Squadron Leader M. 'Mike' Wright, D.F.C., had engine problems whilst over the Alps; nevertheless he continued on to the target and after successfully bombing, a course was set for Spain. After a flight of almost six hours Wyatt managed to crash-land near Gerona. The eight crewmen were duly interned but their release was arranged and they arrived back in the United Kingdom towards the end of January 1943. In the following May, Wyatt was appointed the Commander of 75 (NZ) Squadron followed in May 1944 by the command of No 514 Squadron at Waterbeach after a spell as 3 Group Training Inspector.

Based at Wyton was No 109 Squadron with a mixture of Wellingtons, Ansons and the odd Mosquito, which had been 'attached' to the PFF to pioneer the operational use of *Oboe*, the latest navigational aid. For the last two years 109 had been known as the Special Duties Wireless Squadron and had been trialling various radio and radar aids, especially *Oboe*. The squadron was commanded by Wing Commander H. 'Hal' E. Bufton, brother of Syd; another brother, John, had been killed in action flying Hampdens with 83 Squadron. The Bufton family was just one of numerous families that made a large contribution and sacrifices for the Royal Air Force.

Oboe was really a variation of a system of wireless beams that had been successfully used by the *Luftwaffe* during their night raids of 1940/1, and had been devised in early 1941. In simple terms it was a blind bombing system based on pulses transmitted from two

Squadron Leader M. 'Mike' Wyatt, D.F.C., after his return from Spain. (R.A.F. Museum)

Mosquito BIVs of No 105 Squadron.

ground stations about one hundred miles apart. The aircraft followed a continuous signal from one station (the 'Cat') and the markers or bombs were released at the exact point of intersection from a signal from the second station (the 'Mouse'). There were some limitations to the system; its range was about 280 miles and the stations could only cope with six *Oboe* aircraft in an hour. Only PFF aircraft, mainly Mosquitos, were equipped with *Oboe*; their operational ceiling of 30,000 ft or above extended the range of *Oboe* and this covered the Ruhr. Also their superior speed reduced the time over the bomb run when *Oboe* aircraft were most vulnerable to the German defences.

In late December, 109 Squadron was ready to try out its handful of *Oboe*-equipped Mosquito BIVs under operational conditions. On 22nd/23rd December Wing Commander Hal Bufton led five crews on an *Oboe* attack of a power station at Lutterwade in Holland. Three crews managed to bomb using *Oboe* but the equipment did not function properly in the other two Mosquitos. Another three trials were made with little success. Then on the last night of the year eight Lancasters of 83 Squadron led by two *Oboe* Mosquitos made a trial raid on Düsseldorf, but only one crew was able to use *Oboe* and the result was rather inconclusive. One Lancaster was lost and Pilot Officer L.T. Jackson, D.F.C., R.A.A.F., and his six crewmen were killed.

This was the fifty-seventh PFF aircraft to be lost in action. The Wellington and Stirling squadrons had suffered the heaviest losses, nineteen and twenty-one respectively. The Force's loss rate of 4.2% was slightly more favourable than the Command's overall rate of 4.7%. Nevertheless over three hundred and ten PFF airmen were missing in action, about 30% of them officers, including many very experienced and decorated airmen – two Wing Commanders, five Squadron Leaders and twenty-one Flight Lieutenants. The very nature of the tasks allotted to PFF crews meant that in the future they suffered heavier losses than the rest of the Command and yet despite this very fact crews continued to volunteer to serve as Pathfinders.

Air Marshal Harris, with striking honesty, later described 1942 as 'a year of preparation, in which very little material damage had been done to the enemy which he could not repair from his resources'. It was really a time when he was able to develop the Force's bomber techniques before the long-awaited arrival of the new navigational aids. The strength of his Command had barely increased during the year – some three hundred and forty aircraft and crews: however because of a greater proportion of 'heavies ' (two hundred and sixty) the Command was now able to deliver a far greater and heavier bomb load. What Harris described as 'Bomber Command's main offensive' began with a vengeance in 1943.

'We Guide To Strike': *a fine dramatic painting by Gil Cohen of a Pathfinder crew in action.* (Copyright 2006, Gil Cohen and Vector Fine Arts Prints)

Chapter 7

The Battle of the Ruhr

(JANUARY-JUNE 1943)

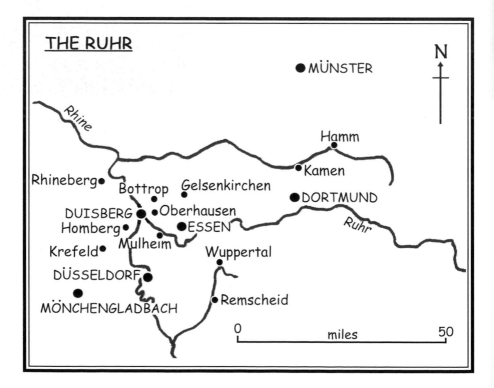

THE RUHR

N

●MÜNSTER

Rhine

Hamm

Rhineberg●

●Kamen

Bottrop Gelsenkirchen

●DORTMUND

DUISBERG● ●Oberhausen

Homberg● ●ESSEN

Ruhr

Krefeld● Mulheim

Wuppertal●

DÜSSELDORF●

●Remscheid

MÖNCHENGLADBACH●

0 miles 50

Flight Lieutenant W.D.G. 'Bill' Wilkes, D.F.M., MiD, (in the centre) and his fellow crew members shortly after returning from an operation.
(Kind permission Myra Wilkes)

Without a shadow of a doubt, 1943 was the most significant period of Bomber Command's long and bitter bombing offensive. During the year it developed into a formidable force; led by PFF aircraft equipped with the two navigational and blind-bombing aids – *Oboe* and *H2S*, it now had the capability of inflicting heavy and extensive damage on a wide range of targets. In March, Harris, with sixty operational squadrons at his command, launched his ferocious and sustained offensive against industrial targets in the Ruhr. These were followed by Operation *Gomorrah* – the devastating fire-raids on Hamburg. In May and August there were the two celebrated and highly publicised operations against the three Dams and the rocket research centre at Peenemünde, which clearly demonstrated the

Command's growing skills in locating and accurately bombing small individual targets. Then, in late August, the offensive against the 'ultimate' target, Berlin, commenced; a vicious and bitter battle that gained momentum over the winter. The quite unprecedented scale of bombing was costly in men and machines, amounting to almost one third of the Command's total wartime losses.

Nevertheless there were many crews that quite amazingly managed to live through and survive these sustained and brutal offensives and such crippling losses. One such airman was Flight Lieutenant W.D.G. 'Bill' Wilkes, D.F.M., MiD; his operational tour lasted from mid-February to late December 1943 – a total of fifty-one missions which entailed over three hundred and twenty-three operational flying hours.

A Halifax pilot awaits the signal to take off.

At the outbreak of the war Bill had been in a reserved occupation, but in April 1941 he volunteered for the R.A.F. and was accepted for flying duties. After pilot training in the U.S.A. he returned to the United Kingdom when the requirement for pilots was no longer so urgent, largely because Bomber Command had dispensed with the second pilot in its crews, but there was a great demand for other crew categories. Bill's civilian experience in telecommunications made him an ideal candidate for bomb aimer and to act as a second pilot if the occasion arose.

After further training Bill and his crew were posted to R.A.F. Syerston, Nottinghamshire, and No 106 squadron, which was then commanded by the celebrated Wing Commander Guy Gibson. His first operation was made on 13th/14th February to the U-boat pens at Lorient. Over the next two months he flew another fifteen operations with 106 Squadron – six targets to the dreaded Ruhr Valley, Nuremberg, Kiel, twice to Italy and also Berlin. At the end of April Bill had been 'headhunted' for the Pathfinder Force, he volunteered, was successful and he joined his previous Squadron Commander, Group Captain John H. Searby, at Wyton, where he had recently taken over the command of No 83 Squadron. It is quite possible that Searby had noted Bill's ability during his short time in command of 106 Squadron.

Bill's first PFF mission was to Duisburg on 12th/13th May 1943 and in early August after completing fourteen PFF operations he was awarded the coveted Pathfinder Badge. His final operation took place on 23rd/24th December to Berlin, the eleventh time he had visited and returned safely from 'The Big City', a quite remarkable record. There are few German and Italian major targets that do not appear on his operational record and he was proud to have taken part in the celebrated Peenemünde raid. For the rest of the war Bill served as a bombing leader instructor and in June 1945 he was 'Mentioned in Despatches' for this training work.

I was privileged to know Bill in his latter years and a more modest and unassuming gentleman (and I use the word in its true meaning) would be difficult to find. Bill claimed, 'I have had a charmed life.' And considering his wartime operational life, who would gainsay that? Sadly, Bill died in January 2005 aged eighty-four years. Like so many of the Command's heroes, he spoke little about his operational experiences but it always deeply saddened him that his official duties had resulted in such a loss of civilian lives.

Before Harris was able to mount his 'main offensive', he was forced by a directive of 1st January 1943 to devote all his resources to the U-boat bases along the French Atlantic coast:

> As a result of the serious increase in the menace of the enemy U-boat operations, the War Cabinet has given approval to a policy of area bombing against the U-boat operational bases on the west coast of France...the order of priority is as follows: Lorient, St Nazaire, Brest, La Pallice. To give effect to this decision you will undertake such an operation on the heaviest scale against Lorient.

A short break from 'the business of war'! A familiar wartime photograph.
(via Bronwen Wilkin)

The most remarkable aspect of this directive was that it sanctioned the 'area bombing' of French targets – how the conduct of the air war had changed. On the night of 14th/15th January Lorient was bombed, the first of no less than eight raids within a space of one month; over 4,000 tons of bombs were dropped and the town was devastated and virtually deserted. Then Harris turned to St Nazaire at the end of February. However, little damage had been sustained by the U-boat pens as they had been protected

DRON
1943.
STER A/c
VETT - CARNAC

by several feet of reinforced concrete, which rendered them virtually bombproof. As Grand Admiral Doenitz remarked, 'No dog or cat is left alive in these towns. Nothing remains but the U-boat pens.' It was not until early April that Air Chief Marshal Harris (he was promoted on 30th March 1943) was released from the directive as photographs had revealed that the U-boat pens were relatively intact.

On 24th January the Allied conference at Casablanca agreed a combined U.S.A.A.F./R.A.F. bombing strategy, which listed essential targets in order of priority – U-boat pens, the German aircraft industry, road/rail transportation and other industrial targets; with the objective of 'undermining the morale of the German people to a point where their capacity for armed resistance is fatally weakened'. Harris viewed this directive as 'a wide range of choice and allowed me to attack pretty well any German industrial city of 100,000 inhabitants and above'. Thus he considered that he had been given the green light to attack targets over the length and breadth of Germany.

During January there were some important changes within the PFF. On the 8th of the month the Force was granted Group status, No 8, with Bennett promoted to Air Commodore, the youngest man to attain Air rank, and within a few months he became an Air Vice-Marshal. Bennett now had aircraft fitted with *Oboe* and *H2S* and was keen to use them operationally. Also he had never hidden his ambition to acquire an all-Lancaster heavy force and the first step of his plan was the conversion of 156 Squadron to Lancasters. The last PFF Wellington sorties were flown on 23rd/24th January to Lorient and three nights later the squadron despatched four Lancasters to the same target – the first of two hundred and thirty Lancaster operations flown by No 156; in fact the squadron would fly the most Lancaster PFF sorties (almost 4,000) and in the process it suffered the heaviest losses, one hundred and four. In May, No 7 Squadron began to exchange its Stirling IIIs for Lancaster IIIs but the faithful Stirlings did not leave the PFF until August.

In ten nights, from 3rd to 13th January, eight *Oboe* experimental raids were mounted to Essen and Duisburg. On the second raid 'skymarker' flares were dropped for the first time. The trial raids were not overly successful but they were just a prelude to the horrors that the citizens of both cities would suffer in the not too distant future. Three nights later (16th/17th) Berlin was the selected target; it had not been bombed for some fourteen months, well before Harris had taken charge of the Command. It was the first occasion that the Command employed an all four-engine bomber force. Berlin was dreaded by crews, a long nine hours flight mostly over enemy territory at a height of 20,000 ft where temperatures could fall below -30°F; furthermore the crews had to face hundreds of searchlights and formidable and intense flak before the long passage home across the inhospitable North Sea. On this operation the PFF dropped 'target indicators' for the first time; they were 250 lb bomb casings packed with pyrotechnic candles, which were ejected at various heights and exploded in a variety of colours – red, green and yellow. According to Guy Gibson, 'these were the bombs that put night bombing on the map'. Quite remarkably just one Lancaster was lost; this may possibly have been due to the higher altitude of the attacking force,

A Lancaster III being loaded with incendiary bombs.

which might have surprised and confused the enemy defences.

On the following night the crews returned to Berlin and because the same route to and from Berlin was used, the night fighters took a heavy toll – twenty-four (12%). Rather unusually the Air Ministry allowed a BBC reporter, Richard Dimbleby, to fly as an observer in a Lancaster of 106 Squadron piloted by Wing Commander Guy Gibson. Dimbleby vividly described the scene over Berlin:

> ...a great silver carpet of fire unrolled itself. It was a retinue of brilliant lights revealing the outlines of the city. Thousands more fire bombs were released and all over the face of the German capital ran streams of fire until the city looked like a garden filled with incandescent flower beds.

This spectacular sight was similar to the response of an airman of 7 Squadron, who spent his nineteenth birthday over Berlin. After landing safely he was asked for his reactions to his first visit to Berlin and replied 'I have never seen such a wonderful display of fireworks'!

The second navigational aid, *H2S*, had been introduced in the previous December when the precious sets were installed into a number of Stirlings of 7 Squadron and Halifaxes of 35 Squadron; this was due in no small measure to Bennett's enthusiasm and support for the new device and during 1943 all PFF squadrons would receive the equipment. *H2S* was an airborne

H2S Mk. IIB installation (left) by the navigator's station on a Lancaster.
(via C. Fairlie)

radar system that could transmit a shadowy image of the ground passing below onto a cathode ray (or Plan Position Indicator), which was carried on the aircraft. An experienced operator using predictions and overlays could analyse and interpret the somewhat confused images that appeared on his screen. There were operational range restrictions but the Germans managed to develop a system to track *H2S* quite accurately and produced a homing device – *Naxos* – which was used by their night fighters.

On 30th/31st January seven Stirlings and six Halifaxes led the first *H2S* operation to Hamburg, although on this occasion its use was not particularly successful despite the fact that Hamburg was close to a coastline and on a prominent river, which should have made it an ideal target for *H2S*. Two nights later it was used against Cologne and an *H2S* Stirling of 7 Squadron crashed in Holland, thus yielding the enemy an *H2S* set on only its second use. A couple of days later Bomber Command announced, 'The problem of accurate navigation under almost any weather conditions is solved by *H2S* when operated by a trained navigator.' This comment was a trifle precipitate but ultimately *H2S*, despite its limitations, proved to be an effective but not, alas, the complete answer to blind bombing and was certainly the most useful aid to navigation and bomb aiming used during the war.

Berlin was targeted for the third time on 1st/2nd March 1943 when a three hundred-strong force was led by *H2S* Pathfinders; the PFF crews experienced difficulties in providing concentrated marking because of the extensive city area, which could not be easily identified on their screens. Nevertheless the operation caused more damage than any previous raid because of the number of aircraft involved and their increased bomb load. Seventeen aircraft were lost (5.6%), two of which belonged to XV Squadron, now commanded by one of its 'old boys' – Wing Commander S.W.B. Menaul, D.F.C. Both aircraft were shot down by night fighters and both were Mark Is although since January the squadron had been the first to receive the new Stirling IIIs, powered by Hercules XVI engines, which had improved the aircraft's speed and ceiling height.

During the raid the captured *H2S* set, which was being reassembled in the Telefunken works, was completely destroyed in the bombing. By

A Lancaster bomb aimer holding the bomb release button.

sheer misfortune later that night a Halifax of 35 Squadron, captained by Squadron Leader P.C. Elliott, D.F.C., was shot down and crashed in Holland thus providing the enemy with an almost intact *H2S* set, enabling them to continue their research without any serious interruption; amongst the six crewmen killed was Flight Sergeant S.L.C. Watts, who had joined the Royal Naval Air Service back in 1916, which suggests that at his death he was in his mid-forties – a fairly rare exception to the youthful image of the Command's aircrew.

During this period one of the most celebrated PFF airmen, probably second only to Bennett himself, was serving in 7 Squadron – T.G. 'Hamish' Mahaddie, D.S.O., D.F.C., A.F.C. & Bar, Czech Military Cross. He was yet another 'Halton brat' who had joined the Service in 1928 and had already completed one operational tour flying Whitleys with 77 Squadron when he joined 7 Squadron for a second tour in August 1942 as a Squadron Leader. By the end of the year he was an acting Wing Commander and in February he received four medals at the same ceremony at Buckingham Palace – a R.A.F. record. On completion of his second tour Mahaddie was seconded to PFF Headquarters as Group Training Inspector, where he was given a free hand to visit bomber squadrons to

Group Captain T.G. 'Hamish' Mahaddie, D.S.O., D.F.C., A.F.C., Bar, CZ.M.C. – 'Bennett's horse thief'.

find and select the best crews for PFF and he became known as 'Bennett's horse thief'! He was utterly dedicated in his promotion of the PFF and the 'Pathfinder Spirit'. In 1944 he was appointed the Station Commander at Warboys, which was then deeply involved in the training of PFF crews. Group Captain Mahaddie retired in 1958 and right up to his death in 1997 at the age of eighty-five, he travelled the world giving talks and lectures on the R.A.F.'s bombing offensive as well as being an active member of several Service associations.

Another remarkable airman joined the PFF in February – Flight Lieutenant

Halifax II (W7710) 'LQ-R' of No 405 (Vancouver) Squadron, appropriately named
Ruhr Valley Express.

A.P. Cranswick, D.F.C., who had volunteered for the R.A.F. in 1939 and by the end of 1940 had completed twenty-nine operations flying Wellingtons with 214 Squadron. He later volunteered for service in the Middle East but returned to join the R.C.A.F.'s 419 (Moose) Squadron before volunteering for the Pathfinders and being posted to 35 Squadron at Graveley, where he would complete his third operational tour.

By the beginning of March 1943, Harris felt free to devote all his resources to industrial targets in the Ruhr, an all-out offensive that he aptly named 'The Battle of the Ruhr'. He had been planning such a major offensive almost since he had taken over the Command. From early March until late July, twenty-eight operations were mounted with Essen receiving six raids, Duisburg five, Bochum three and Düsseldorf, Dortmund, Wuppertal and Gelsenkirchen being targeted on two nights. It was an awesome demonstration of the power of Bomber Command, which lay waste large areas of the Ruhr. Also during the five months other targets well away from the Ruhr were bombed – such as Nuremberg, Stettin, Turin and even Pilsen in Czechoslovakia. These were rated as 'nuisance raids' but they ensured that the Germans could not concentrate their night fighters and flak defences in the defence of the Ruhr.

The outstanding success of the Battle of the Ruhr was achieved at no small loss, almost 3,800 airmen missing in action and over six hundred and forty aircraft destroyed. Although overall the casualty rate at 4.9% was just below the 'tolerable' or sustainable limit, this rate was well exceeded in several individual operations. Such heavy losses could not have been borne over so prolonged a period but for the ready and ample supply of newly trained crews arriving almost daily from the twenty-two O.T.U.s. During this period of intense operational activity and high losses, morale on the squadrons did not waver, the crews were well aware of the successful results of their nightly ordeals. One historian has remarked that 'a special brand of courage was necessary of its airmen in continuing to fly against such formidable defences that were in place in the Ruhr', and, one might add, in the face of the continual loss of friends and colleagues.

The Battle opened on 5th/6th March when, perhaps needless to say, Essen was the target for over four hundred and forty aircraft. It was the twenty-first time Essen had been bombed and during the operation the Command flew its 100,000th sortie. This operation was the most successful so far, over

Total devastation – the Krupps factories in Essen, 1945. (Via H. Hughes)

A Lancaster crew en route *to board their aircraft.*

one hundred and sixty acres of the city were destroyed and the Krupps factories sustained heavy damage. Some of the markers dropped by *Oboe* Mosquitos fell within seventy-five yards of the targets. In the words of Harris: 'This was the precise moment when Bomber Command's main offensive began; the moment of the first major attack on an objective in Germany by means of *Oboe*.'

During the next five weeks the crews returned to Essen on three nights. Duisburg was also their target on four nights. Every operation to the Ruhr was led by *Oboe* Mosquitos of 109 Squadron and both Harris and Bennett acknowledged the immense contribution made by the Mosquito crews. Harris described the *Oboe* Mosquito as 'the consummate and indispensable pathfinder'; furthermore they accomplished their tasks with a quite remarkably low casualty rate, the first *Oboe* Mosquito lost in action went missing on the Duisburg operation on 26th/27th April. Flight Lieutenant L. Ackland, D.F.C., and Warrant Officer F. Stoats, R.C.A.F., were presumed missing in action, their bodies were never found and like so very many of their colleagues their names appear on the fine Runnymede Memorial at Cooper's Hill in Surrey.

By the end of April over 3,400 sorties had been flown mainly to Duisburg and Essen, one hundred and fifty aircraft lost in action and another seventy severely damaged. The PFF squadrons lost sixteen crews and on one night

(3rd/4th April), when Essen was the target for the third time, 83 Squadron lost three crews, which proved to be the squadron's heaviest loss during 1943. It would suffer fewer losses than other Lancaster squadrons despite its PFF role and for two months during the summer it survived many operations without a single casualty. When Goebbels, the German Propaganda Minister, visited Essen after this third raid he noted in his diary that 'the damage was colossal and indeed ghastly', and yet Essen would be bombed another three times during the Battle.

In April, XV Squadron found itself on the move again when it was ordered to vacate Bourn for one of the new PFF squadrons transferred to 8 Group. On the 14th of the month the squadron left for Mildenhall, Suffolk, thus severing its links with Cambridgeshire that dated back to December 1939. Four days later No 97 (Straits Settlements) Squadron brought its Lancasters from Woodhall Spa, Lincolnshire. Under its Commander, Wing Commander G.D. Jones, D.F.C., the crews began their training on PFF techniques and they completed their first PFF operation on 26th/27th April, when all eight crews arrived back safely from Duisburg.

The other addition to 8 Group was No 405 (Vancouver) Squadron, which arrived at Gransden Lodge from Leeming, Yorkshire. It had been the first R.C.A.F. squadron to join Bomber Command in April 1941. Its arrival brought one of the most charismatic PFF Commanders, Group Captain J.E. 'Johnnie' Fauquier, D.S.O. & 2 Bars, D.F.C., who had previously commanded the squadron in 1942. One of only eight airmen to be awarded a second bar to his D.S.O., Fauquier was an outstanding and inspirational leader and his many exploits earned him the title 'The King of the Pathfinders'. The squadron was equipped with Halifax IIs and eleven crews left for Duisburg on 26th/27th April. Sadly one crew failed to return – seven were R.C.A.F. airmen, one of whom, Flight Sergeant S. Sleeth, was an American from Detriot, one of many American citizens that served with the Royal Canadian Air Force.

During the month another unit joined the burgeoning PFF – No 1409 (Meteorological) Flight, which had been formed to undertake long-distance weather reconnaissance patrols *(Pampas)* over targets to be bombed the following night. The Flight was equipped with Mosquito IVs and the first sortie left Oakington on 2nd April for Brittany prior to the Command's last operation to St Nazaire and Lorient. In May the Flight began to receive its first Mark IXs and on 14th June one was shot down by two Focke-Wulf 190s at a height of 28,000 ft. Both crew members baled out and the navigator, Pilot Officer R. Taylor, managed to evade capture. The Flight had a most remarkable wartime record completing over 1,360 sorties for the loss of three Mosquitos.

After the hectic pace of operations during April especially, the crews must have felt that the month of May offered some blessed relief. There were no less than twenty-two nights when the main force was not in action, the longest being a nine-day break in the middle of the month because of the full moon period. Although many crews felt that all the anxiety of waiting to hear that there was 'an ops tonight' was harder to bear; as a navigator of 35 Squadron later recalled, 'we had established a daily routine whereby we tried not to dwell on what the night might bring'. During these breaks in operations most crews were given a week's leave, which in theory was normally granted every six weeks.

Nevertheless during May 1943 some of the most successful operations were mounted to Ruhr targets, including the famous Dambusters raid. On the 4th/5th Dortmund was attacked for the first time by almost six hundred aircraft, the largest four-engine bomber force so far. The PFF marking was good and the damage was severe, mainly caused by fire; as one crewman remembered, 'the fires were unbelievable'. Twenty-two (5.2%) aircraft were shot down, mainly by night fighters, but the crews returning to their bases found that many were closed due to fog and sadly ten aircraft were either

Mosquito IX (ML897) of No 1409 (Met) Flight.

Group Captain John Searby, D.F.C., Commander of No 83 Squadron.

abandoned or crash landed, making the night's losses rather high at 6.8%. The PFF squadrons lost seven aircraft with Wing Commander J.R. Gillman, D.F.C., and his crew of 83 Squadron killed over the target. He had been the Squadron Commander since February.

Four days later Group Captain John Searby, D.F.C., arrived at Wyton to take over command of the squadron. It was a case of the return of a local hero as he had been born in nearby Whittlesey. Searby had been flying since 1935 and was another of the countless number of Second World War airmen that had entered the Service via Halton Apprentice School. He was considered one of the foremost navigation experts in the Service and had served as an instructor before being posted to Ferry Command. In 1942 he joined 106 Squadron for his full operational tour under the legendary Guy Gibson, and took over the squadron when Gibson left to command 617 Squadron; indeed he had led 106 Squadron over Dortmund. Searby would act as the 'Master Bomber' on the famous Peenemünde raid in August.

After a break of seven nights Duisburg was the target for the fifth time in two months. On this occasion the PFF marking was rated as 'near perfect' and in just forty-five minutes over 1,600 tons of bombs were dropped, inflicting such severe damage that Duisburg was not attacked again in any great strength until 1944. Of the thirty-four aircraft (5.9%) lost in action, two came from 156 Squadron. One was captained by Squadron Leader L. Verdon-Roe, D.F.C., who was related to the family that had built the Lancaster; he was also one of the last surviving 'veterans' from the old Wellington days and the fifth Flight Commander to go missing in two months.

Perhaps the outstanding success of the Battle of the Ruhr was the operation to Wuppertal on 29th/30th May. It was about fifteen miles south-east of Essen and had been amalgamated from two towns – Barmen and Elberfeld. Over seven hundred and ten aircraft attacked in three waves and because of the excellence of the PFF marking the concentration of bombing over the Barmen area was so accurate that a small form of what would later be known as a 'firestorm' destroyed over 60% of the built-up area. As Bomber Command's Report No 340 stated: 'The fire-raising technique was effectively employed, as a complement to ground marking, resulting in the best concentration yet achieved by the Pathfinder Force. Immense damage was caused in the town, covering over 1,000 acres and affecting 113 industrial concerns, as well as totally disrupting the transport system and public utilities.' Of the thirty-eight aircraft missing, four came from

Lancasters of No 156 Squadron leaving R.A.F. Warboys in 1943. Original painting by Colin Doggett. (Kind permission Colin Doggett)

35 Squadron at Graveley, all shot down by night fighters – twenty-nine airmen missing in action, including Flight Lieutenant W.A. Tetley, who had only just arrived at Graveley to take over as the Squadron Bombing Leader. After this operation Harris sent a message to all the squadrons taking part:

> Yes, in 1939, Goering promised that not a single bomb would reach the Ruhr. Congratulations on delivering the first 100,000 tons on Germany The next 100,000 if he waits for them, will be even bigger and better bombs delivered even more accurately and in much shorter time.

Despite the reduced scale of operations during May the Command's losses were steadily mounting. Over two hundred and seventy aircraft had been lost during the month with just over 1,700 airmen missing in action, although about 20% survived as prisoners of war and six managed to evade capture.

Perhaps one of the more remarkable statistics of the R.A.F during the Second World War was that over 2,380 airmen successfully evaded capture in Western Europe after their aircraft had been shot down over enemy-occupied countries and the majority of these were Bomber Command aircrew. During 1943 alone some two hundred and fifty airmen evaded and it was the normal practice that when they finally arrived back in the United Kingdom they were awarded the D.F.C. or D.F.M. respectively. It was, of course, official policy that it was the duty of every airman to attempt to escape from captivity or to evade it.

Every bomber station had ample information on evasion and escape and regular lectures were given to crews on the various procedures; occasionally these talks were given by airmen who had successfully evaded. Before every operation each member of crew was issued with an escape or survival pack, which was handed back on their safe return. The pack contained rations for forty-eight hours, a rudimentary compass, milk, water purifying and Benzedrine tablets, soap, razor, needle and thread and a detailed waterproof map printed on silk. An amount of foreign currency, normally equivalent to £12, was issued and small passport-size photographs were sown into uniforms to produce forged identity documents.

A few evaders managed unaided but the vast majority were assisted by the thousands of courageous men and women – the 'helpers' – of the many 'escape lines' that had been established in Belgium, France and Holland; most of these admirable organisations operated under the guidance and support of MI9, the department of the Military Intelligence Service devoted to escape and evasion, which had been set up under Major (later Brigadier) N.R. Crockatt, D.S.O., M.C., in December 1939. It was claimed that by June 1944 the escape lines had been so developed that an airman shot down over Belgium or France had a fifty-fifty chance of successfully evading capture. Nevertheless as with every aspect of operational flying, a good measure of luck played a major role.

The first PFF airmen to evade in 1943 were five from a Halifax II of 35 Squadron on 13th/14th February, which the crew abandoned over France after a raid to Lorient; only ten days earlier they had survived a crash-landing on return to Graveley. In fact the squadron had the highest number of evaders during the year, no less than twenty-five, closely followed by 7 Squadron with twenty-one.

The most celebrated evader of 35 Squadron was Flight Lieutenant D. Julian Slade, D.F.C., whose Halifax II was shot down by a night fighter over Holland on 12th/13th May during a raid on Duisburg; two of the crew were killed and four taken prisoner. Slade covered over 1,250 miles by foot and by bike passing through Germany, Holland, Belgium, Andorra and Spain. He arrived in Gibraltar on 5th August and reached Liverpool six days

Squadron Leader Julian Slade, D.S.O., Bar, D.F.C., (third from left) of No 35 Squadron with his crew and ground crew. To his right is Flight Lieutenant Gordon Carter, D.F.C., like Slade a successful evader.

later. He was recommended for an 'immediate' D.S.O. in September.

Slade, who was a Canadian, was a brilliant pilot and fine leader, attributes that he showed on 20th/21st December when, waiting to land at Graveley, a target indicator caught fire. Slade ordered the crew to bale out; unfortunately one of the crew's parachutes had been destroyed by the flames, so Slade calmly landed the blazing aircraft and he and the other crewman managed to escape only seconds before the aircraft exploded. For this action Squadron Leader Slade was awarded an 'immediate' bar to his D.S.O. – his navigator, Flight Lieutenant Gordon H.F. Carter, D.F.C., R.C.A.F., who baled out safely had been one of the five airmen that successfully evaded back in February. Sadly less than two months later, 19th/20th February 1944, whilst en route to Leipzig, Slade's Halifax III was shot down by a night fighter and crashed. He was severely injured and two weeks later he died of his wounds. However, Squadron Leader Gordon Taylor, then the squadron's Navigation Leader, baled out and, although he evaded capture for a while, he was finally taken prisoner.

One of 7 Squadron's evaders, Sergeant Donald V. Smith, R.C.A.F., made the first successful escape from Denmark. On 20th/21st April 1943 he was the only survivor of an eight-man Stirling crew shot down after a raid to Stettin. He walked across Zealand for a day and a night and slept in a barn before meeting a friendly farmer, who gave him food and some money (he had been issued with French francs). Then by mere chance he encountered some members of the Danish Resistance who took him across to Sweden in a rubber boat that they had stolen from the Germans! After a brief spell of internment Smith was back in the United Kingdom by July when he was awarded the D.F.M. Such fine and courageous airmen as Slade, Carter and Smith were the backbone of the PFF and they and thousands like them made the PFF such a formidable and successful force.

In May 1943 a new bomber airfield opened in Cambridgeshire, West Wickham, close to the boundary with Suffolk, although within a few months it was renamed Wratting Common. The airfield was allocated to No 3 Group and on the last day of the month the Stirlings of 90 Squadron arrived from Ridgewell, Essex. The squadron had experienced a rather peripatetic wartime existence; West Wickham was its seventh but not last wartime station. Furthermore it had been the only R.A.F. squadron to be equipped with Flying Fortresses, which proved to be a less than successful experiment. On the 21st/22nd the squadron lost its first crew from West Wickham and then in just three raids it lost another five crews; in a matter of five nights forty-six airmen went missing in action.

There was no let up in the Command's relentless onslaught of the Ruhr. During the last week of June alone four major operations were despatched to Ruhr targets and one to Cologne. Throughout the Battle the PFF squadrons had been sustaining a steady and regular loss of highly experienced crews; many of their aircraft were now equipped with *H2S* and coded 'Y'. These last operations in June exacted a heavy toll of PFF crews – twenty-seven in just seven nights. One raid to Krefeld on 21st/22nd June was highly successful as most of the 2,300 tons of bombs fell within three miles of the city centre and almost half of it was burnt out.

Unfortunately the raid proved to be especially costly; out of the forty-four aircraft lost (6.2%) no less than fourteen were from 8 Group. The operation had been carried out just before the end of 'the moon period' and in the clear skies at least thirty aircraft fell to night fighters. It proved to be a disastrous night for 35 Squadron; six out of its nineteen Halifaxes failed to return to Graveley, the squadron's heaviest loss of the war. There was perhaps a small consolation for the squadron – Flight Lieutenant Alex Cranswick, D.F.C., survived and thus completed his ninety-sixth operation. For this almost unbelievable feat he was awarded the DSO and was seconded to the PFF Headquarters Staff. The night was also traumatic for 7 Squadron at Oakington, four of their Stirlings were lost.

Three nights later (24th/25th) when the Elberfeld area of Wuppertal was almost completely flattened, 7 Squadron lost another three crews including its Squadron Commander, Wing Commander R.G. Barrell, D.S.O., D.F.C. & Bar, who although he was only twenty-three years old was on his sixtieth operation; in fact his crew totalled no less than three hundred and eight operations between them. Like so many brave and courageous captains, Barrell remained with his stricken aircraft until all the crew had baled out but sadly his parachute failed to open. Another four PFF crews were lost on the night, two from 156 Squadron and both captained by R.A.A.F. airmen with a total loss of fourteen crewmen.

It is difficult to imagine that the PFF could replace so many talented, experienced and brave airmen that had been lost during the Battle but replace them they did. Mahaddie ensured that there was no shortage of volunteers, new names came forward and took over their mantle and the Pathfinder Force went from strength to strength. As yet the Battle of the Ruhr was not quite over, Hamburg beckoned and the Command's second major offensive of the year – the Battle of Berlin – was also close at hand.

Chapter 8

Hamburg, Peenemünde and Berlin

JULY-DECEMBER 1943

In retrospect the second half of 1943 can be viewed as the pinnacle of Bomber Command throughout its long and bitter war. However, as the year came to a close it was clear that its crews were engaged in a desperate battle of attrition with the *Luftwaffe*'s night fighter force, which several historians have likened to the First World War Battle of Passchendaele, and as the Command's losses mounted steadily it would appear that they were losing this particular battle.

Towards the end of June a celebrated squadron, No 75 (NZ), moved into the new station at Mepal. It had been formed in April 1940 as the only night-bomber squadron from New Zealand and was now an experienced and battle-hardened unit, having flown almost 3,500 sorties and lost over one hundred aircraft in the process. The arrival of its Stirling IIIs marked the return to Cambridgeshire of Wing Commander M. 'Mike' Wright (noted earlier) as its Squadron Commander; the first operation from Mepal took place on 3rd/4th July to Cologne.

In July 1943 the third new bomber station to open in the county was at Witchford, about two miles south-west of Ely, and it was allocated to 3 Group. During 1943 the Command's operational stations increased from one hundred and five to one hundred and twenty-eight, mainly due to the new squadrons that were formed. No 196 Squadron arrived in late July and its crews were in the process of exchanging their Wellington Xs for Stirling IIIs, perhaps a little belatedly considering that the aircraft was nearing its end as a main force bomber. Indeed the squadron's time at Witchford proved to be rather brief as it moved out in late November to serve in Transport Command.

Since late May the Group Commanders had been aware that Air Chief Marshal Harris was planning a major offensive against Hamburg. It was the largest port in Europe, Germany's second biggest city and a major centre of U-boat construction. It had already suffered nearly one hundred raids but nothing could prepare it for the terrific onslaught it experienced during late July and early August. The Battle of Hamburg, four nights of intensive bombing, was probably the most successful series of operations ever undertaken by Bomber Command.

Window *released by Lancasters.*

A heavily damaged Stirling III that still arrived back safely. (via J. Adams)

Operation *Gomorrah*, as was its rather macabre code-name, commenced on 24th/25th July when almost eight hundred aircraft, flying at various heights and in a continuous stream almost two hundred miles long, set out for Hamburg. *Window* was used for the first time: this was small metallic paper strips measuring 27 cms by 2 cms, which were designed to confuse and counter the German radar defences. They were tied in bundles of 2,200, which were released by the crews via the flare chutes every minute both on the way out and on the return. It certainly worked because only twelve aircraft were lost (1.5%), the lowest loss on a major operation for at least eighteen months. In a matter of fifty minutes over 2,200 tons of bombs rained down on the city.

Anxious to take full advantage of *Window*, the following night Harris selected Essen for the sixth time during the Battle of the Ruhr. Over six hundred and twenty aircraft delivered a fierce onslaught with over 2,000 tons of bombs dropped in barely fifty minutes. Nine *Oboe* Mosquitos accurately placed ground markers and Essen sustained more damage in one night than in all the previous raids put together. Brigadier-General Fred Anderson of the U.S.A.A.F. flew in a Lancaster of 83 Squadron and remarked that the view of the burning city was one of the most impressive sights he had seen. The Krupps' factories were so severely damaged that when Doktar Gustav Krupps saw the destruction the following morning he had a stroke from which he never recovered. Losses were minimal, at least when compared with previous Essen operations – twenty-six (2.9%) – although once again more Stirlings were missing (6.7%), one each from 75 and 90 Squadrons; both aircraft ditched in the North Sea on their return but with no survivors.

After a break of one night over seven hundred and eighty crews were detailed for the second Hamburg operation, which proved even more destructive. Over 2,520 tons of bombs were dropped, which created the first man-made 'firestorm', resulting in heavy damage and large civilian casualties. After this raid over one million people fled the city and did not return. The third raid, on the 29th/30th, created further widespread fires – as one crew member recalled, 'the sight below was far beyond all human imagination'.

Air Vice-Marshal Bennett had managed to acquire another Mosquito squadron, No 105, which was operating from Marham, Norfolk. On 4th July 109 Squadron left Wyton to join it at Marham and was replaced by another Mosquito squadron, 139, making a welcome return to Cambridgeshire and more precisely Wyton; it was commanded by Wing Commander R. W. Reynolds, D.S.O., Bar, D.F.C., a celebrated 'Mossie' pilot. The crews had been given the task of flying diversion or 'spoof' raids designed to confuse the enemy's defences as to the main force's target. The squadron would also pioneer the bombing operations of what Bennett named his 'Light Night Striking Force' (LNSF).

The Battle of the Ruhr drew to a close on 30th/31st July 1943 with a shattering attack on Remscheid, which was considered one of the most successful of the whole offensive. The town, on the southern edge of the Ruhr, had not previously been bombed. The target was expertly marked by *Oboe* Mosquitos and the relatively small force of two hundred and seventy-three aircraft created mayhem. Of the fifteen aircraft lost, eight were Stirlings (10%) – two from Mepal and one from West Wickham. Despite their growing losses compared with Lancasters and Halifaxes, the crews felt that they belonged to 'Rolls-Royce squadrons' as opposed to 'the mass produced Lancs and Hallies', but however laudable were such views, the losses sustained in the coming months belied their faith in their aircraft.

The final Hamburg raid on 2nd/3rd August was the least successful. Largely due to heavy thunderstorms over Germany, many crews were forced to turn back or bombed alternative targets, but really there was hardly anything left standing in Hamburg to bomb. In the four operations over 3,000 sorties had been flown, almost 8,000 tons of bombs dropped for the loss of eighty-seven aircraft (2.8%) and four hundred and fifty-four airmen killed and sixty-five taken prisoner. Three-quarters of the city had been destroyed and it was estimated that some 50,000 civilians had been killed. Such was the utter devastation that Hamburg was not bombed again until a year later. It had been an awesome demonstration of the power and strength of Bomber

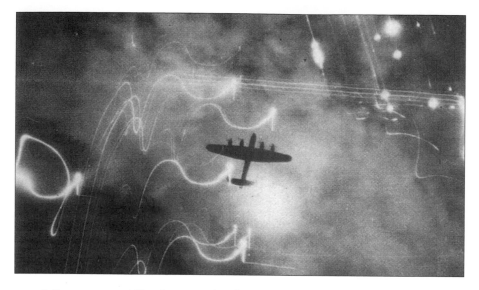

A Lancaster over Hamburg – 2nd/3rd August 1943. (Imperial War Museum)

Command and according to Colonel Adolf Galland, Germany's celebrated fighter pilot:

> ...a wave of terror radiated from the suffering city and spread throughout Germany. Appalling details of the great fires were recounted...In every large town people said 'What happened to Hamburg yesterday can happen to us tomorrow'...After Hamburg in the wide circle of the political and military command could be heard the words: 'The war is lost...'

Air Vice-Marshal Bennett later wrote: 'Towards the end of July 1943 we achieved what I regard as the greatest victory of the war, land, sea or air. This victory was the Battle of Hamburg. The result was staggering.'

These raids ushered in a most active operational time for the crews; in fact August was the busiest month of 1943. Before Harris could direct his force to the 'ultimate' target – Berlin – he was compelled by political pressure to attack Italian targets in an attempt to hasten Italy's exit from the war. It could well be argued that this offensive had the desired effect when Italy signed an Armistice on 3rd September.

In six raids to Genoa, Turin and Milan over 1,300 sorties were flown for the loss of just nineteen aircraft (1.4%). These operations were memorable to the crews in several respects, the light flak and relatively few night fighters they encountered, the long duration of the flights and more especially the magnificent views of the Alps. They were perhaps notable for the use of a MC (Master of Ceremonies) over Turin on the 7th/8th; effectively a senior and experienced pilot, who controlled the marking and bombing throughout the raid by means of VHR Radio/Transmission. The airman chosen for this special task was Group Captain Searby, D.F.C., of 83 Squadron, and it proved to be a trial for the same role he performed over Peenemünde days later. After Turin and Milan were bombed on the 12th/13th, Flight Sergeant Arthur L. Aaron, D.F.M., a Stirling pilot with 218 Squadron, was posthumously awarded the Victoria Cross for his heroic actions on this operation. It has been described as 'one of the bravest Victoria Crosses of the air war'; Aaron was only twenty-one years old and flying his nineteenth operation.

Five nights later (17th/18th August) Harris launched the attack on the German V2 rocket research establishment at Peenemünde on the Baltic coast. This operation, code-named *Hydra*, was notable in several respects. It was the first time that the Command had attempted a major precision raid at night on such a small target; it was the first time that an MC or 'Master Bomber' controlled a full-scale operation; and because there were three specific aiming points – the experimental station, the rocket factory and the living quarters – the PFF would attempt to move the marking whilst the raid was in progress; these crews were called 'shifters'. Group Captain Searby would control almost six hundred aircraft and the importance of the operation was impressed on all the crews at their briefings: 'If you don't knock out this target tonight, it will be laid on again tomorrow and every night until the job is done...Tonight they won't be expecting you, but from then they'll be expecting you.' The operation was carried out in bright moonlight, deliberately so to increase the chance of success and the bombing would be at 8,000 ft, additional factors that added tension to this 'biggie'.

Eight Mosquitos of 139 Squadron were sent to Berlin in an attempt to lure the night fighters away. Searby was over the target just one minute early and for the next hour he remained directing the three waves of bombers. His actions were later described as 'one of the greatest acts of individual bravery of the war'. The diversion had succeeded in drawing off the night fighters, at least for the first two waves but they returned in time for the third wave and most of the forty aircraft shot down came from this wave, largely made up by R.C.A.F. squadrons of 6 Group. It was the first night that the *Luftwaffe*

The V-2 Rocket Assembly Hall and the workers' housing area at Peenemünde after the remarkable precision raid.

used their new *Schräge-Musik* (literally 'slanted music') weapons, twin upward-firing cannons fitted to Me.110s.

The PFF escaped relatively unscathed, although a Lancaster of 405 Squadron was the first to fall when the crew strayed south of the planned route. Some 1,800 tons of bombs were dropped and much of the research station was destroyed, causing serious delay to the enemy's rocket programme. This spectacular operation was probably the apogee of the Command's

Flight Sergeant S. Mason (second left) and his crew of 90 Squadron being de-briefed at Wratting Common after an operation to Berlin on 23rd/24th August 1943.

successes in 1943 and an 'immediate' D.S.O. was awarded to Group Captain Searby.

It is unlikely that Harris wanted to start his Berlin offensive as early as August (in his *Bomber Offensive* he wrote: 'The Battle of Berlin, as it came to be known, began on the night of November 18th-19th...'), nevertheless on 19th August Winston Churchill urged him to attack Berlin, and on the 23rd/24th Harris duly obliged. A 'maximum effort' was called for and seven hundred and nineteen crews were briefed. Many of them had not been on a Berlin operation, so there was 'a moment of excitement and fear' on being told that 'The Big City', as the crews named Berlin, was the 'target for tonight'. As one crewman recalled, 'Although we knew that it would be a long, hard and dangerous operation, it was the one target that every crew member wanted to see in his log book for the prestige that name gave it.'

The importance of this operation, certainly as far as the PFF was concerned, can be shown by the fact that three Station Commanders in 8 Group – Group Captains N.H. Freeson at Bourn, B.V. Robinson at Graveley and A.H. Willetts from Oakington – flew on the mission, and only one returned. For the first time a Master Bomber was used over a German city target – Wing Commander J.E. Fauquier, the Commander of 405 Squadron;

he was selected because: 'He had the ability to impose his will. He was a bright, hard fellow, who certainly would have made the Master Bomber method work if anyone could.'

The operation was only partially successful; the *H2S* marking fell short of the target area and much of the bombing fell outside the city. The enemy's defences were particularly ferocious and sixty-two aircraft (8.6%) were lost – the heaviest loss of the war so far; over five hundred and twenty airmen missing in action in just one night and many were highly experienced, especially those serving with the PFF. Group Captain Robinson, D.S.O., D.F.C., Bar, A.F.C., was killed along with his crew of 35 Squadron and all but one was decorated. Group Captain Willetts, D.S.O., and his crew of 7 Squadron survived as prisoners of war. Flight Lieutenant I.C. 'Brian' Slade, D.F.C., of 83 Squadron was on his fifty-ninth operation although he was only twenty-one years old and was affectionately known as 'The Boy Slade' (just one of several unrelated 'Slades' to serve with distinction in the PFF) – there was just one survivor out of his crew; in total the crew had flown three hundred and thirty operations and their *average* age was twenty-one. Twelve PFF crews were lost on this night, two staff officers at the PFF

Stirling IIIs of 90 Squadron line up at Wratting Common, August 1943.

Headquarters, Squadron Leaders, J.N. Forrest, D.S.O., D.F.C., and E.H. Parrott, were killed along with the crew of one of the two 97 Squadron Lancasters that failed to return to Bourn. Another five crews operating from Cambridgeshire airfields were lost, three from 75 (NZ) Squadron and two from 90 Squadron. 'The Big City' had begun to exact its toll of the Command's young and also senior airmen.

The second Berlin operation eight nights later (31st August/1st September) was another costly operation, when out of six hundred and twenty-two aircraft despatched, forty-seven (7.6%) failed to return. It was the first night that the crews recorded the *Luftwaffe*'s use of 'fighter flares' to illuminate the bombers. As one crewman recalled, 'it was like suddenly coming out of a dark lane into a brightly lit street...

Group Captain Johnnie Fauquier, D.S.O., 2 Bars, D.F.C. (centre) with Air Vice-Marshal Bennett (left) beside Ruhr Express.

it was a blinding light'. They certainly had the desired effect – over two-thirds of the bombers were shot down by night fighters. No 97 Squadron lost one crew captained by Wing Commander, K. H. Burns, D.F.C.; he was a most experienced pilot and a fine leader, who had been the Master Bomber on a Nuremberg operation a few nights earlier. Burns was taken prisoner and because he had lost a hand in the explosion, he was repatriated in 1944; after having an artificial hand fitted he returned to flying as a transport pilot. Seventeen Stirlings were lost on the night (16%) and with heavy losses (sixteen) in the first Berlin raid, they were omitted from the next Berlin operation. No 75 Squadron at Mepal lost five crews. One of its Stirlings was hit by bombs over the target area, but as Stirlings operated at a lower height they were always vulnerable to such unfortunate accidents. After this night one and a half million women and children were evacuated from Berlin.

'R5868' Queenie *at Wyton in May 1943 with its* Devils in the Air *insignia and Flight Lieutenant Rick Garvey and his crew.* (via A. Bowen)

The operations during August 1943 had taken a heavy toll on the Command and perhaps more especially on the PFF. Forty Pathfinder aircraft had been lost in action, virtually equivalent to two squadrons. No 35 Squadron suffered the heaviest losses – ten Halifaxes – followed by eight from 405; it would be almost the end of the year before the much improved Halifax III reached 35 Squadron, whereas 405 began to exchange its Halifax IIs for Lancasters in September. Rather appropriately they were supplied with the first Lancasters to be built in Canada by the Victory Aircraft Company, powered by Packard-built Merlin engines and designated Mark Xs. The first, KB700, *Ruhr Express*, completed just two operations from Gransden Lodge before being transferred to another Canadian squadron, 419 (Moose).

In the previous month perhaps the most famous Lancaster of the war, R5868 OL-Q *Queenie*, completed its last operational sortie (the sixty-seventh) from Wyton on 14th/15th July to Milan, piloted by Flight Lieutenant R.J. 'Rick' Garvey, D.F.C. Since its arrival at 83 Squadron back in June 1942, one D.S.O., five D.F.C.s and two D.F.M.s had been awarded to airmen whilst flying in *Queenie*; sad to relate, seven of those airmen were killed in 1943.

Queenie moved to 467 (R.A.A.F.) Squadron at Bottesford where it survived the war, having completed over one hundred and thirty operations. In March 1972 it went on display at the R.A.F. Museum, Hendon, resplendent with its bomb symbols and Hermann Goering's vain boast: 'No enemy planes will fly over the Reich territory'!

The third Berlin raid on 3rd/4th September was perhaps significant in that only Lancasters (three hundred and sixteen) took part and it was also the fourth anniversary of the outbreak of war. The *H2S* marking showed some improvement and the whole raid lasted only sixteen minutes but the centre of the city escaped serious damage. Nevertheless twenty Lancasters were lost with over one hundred and forty airmen; of these one hundred and thirty were killed. This illustrates the fact that, however excellent the Lancaster was as a heavy bomber, its crews suffered a higher *fatal* casualty rate than both Halifaxes and Stirlings, largely due to its heavier bomb load and the poorly designed escape hatches.

The three operations had shown an average loss rate of 7.6%, considerably more than other German targets, which forced Harris to abandon his Berlin offensive for almost three months. It was hoped that by then the improved *H2S* Mark III would be available, which was based on shorter wave lengths and in theory should provide a clearer target image. Also a new Bomber Command Group, No 100, was being formed with two specific roles – the operation of Radio-Countermeasures to jam the enemy's night fighters' communications and Mosquito night fighters to seek out the enemy's fighter force by using *Serrate*, a device which picked up their radar emissions.

A Lancaster crew of 83 Squadron at Wyton receives the green 'go' signal to take off.

A publicity photograph of a Flight Engineer.

During September and October 1943 several important targets – Mannheim, Stuttgart, Frankfurt, Munich and Leipzig – were sought out by Bomber Command and although they were all outside the range of *Oboe*, they were not so heavily defended as either Berlin or the Ruhr valley. But Harris selected two targets for special treatment – Hanover and Kassel.

On 22nd/23rd September Hanover received its first raid for two years, the first of four in less than a month. The PFF marking was not very accurate largely due to strong winds over the target. Five nights later (27th/28th) the crews returned and once again the PFF marking was less than successful. So on 8th/9th October over five hundred crews found themselves bound for Hanover again. On this night the marking was precise, which resulted in a heavy and concentrated attack on the centre of the city; it proved to be the city's heaviest raid of the war. Twenty-seven aircraft (4.5%) were lost but all the Wellingtons returned safely. This was the last occasion that Wellingtons operated in the main force – four years of action as a front-line bomber had come to an end. During the final Hanover raid on 18th/19th October, the Command lost its 5,000th aircraft in action, over 90% of these by night. This raid was not successful, adverse weather resulting in scattered marking and bombing.

Harris wrote to Bennett about the poor standard of marking in these raids. Bennett replied at some length and largely blamed the weather; he did, however, point out that far from his Force being made up from 'the best crews available', over one third had no operational practice when posted to the PFF. He also commented that in February the average experience of his captains was thirty-two operations but had now fallen to twenty. The heavy losses suffered by the PFF during the summer had greatly denuded his Force of seasoned crews and leaders. He requested that in future 'no direct entry freshmen crews' should be posted to his squadrons, to which Harris agreed, albeit somewhat reluctantly. The loss of so many experienced airmen would be a constant problem for the PFF, especially during the winter of 1943/4.

The two attacks on Kassel during October 1943 showed the problems faced by PFF crews marking by *H2S*. On 3rd/4th the marking was poor, largely due to a heavy ground haze and it was also thought that the Germans had used 'decoy markers' to attract the main force away from the city centre. However, when the crews returned on 22nd/23rd the targets were clear and the marking was deadly accurate. It brought forth such a ferocious onslaught that much of Kassel was devastated, the heaviest damage inflicted on any target since the Hamburg raids and, in fact, such heavy destruction would not be repeated on a German target until well into 1944.

Some French targets could on occasions cause heavy casualties, as 35 Squadron found to their cost on 10th/11th November when the marshalling yards at Cannes in the south of France were the target for one hundred and fifty-three aircraft, predominantly Halifaxes. Cannes was an important rail junction on the coastal route to Italy. On this operation five Halifaxes failed to return, three from Graveley. Two were shot down by night fighters on their return flight. The third, captained by Pilot Officer J.R. Petrie-Andrews, D.F.C., D.F.M., reached the target on three engines and after bombing he continued south before successfully ditching off Sardinia and all of the crew were rescued. Of the other missing airmen no fewer than six managed to evade capture, evidence of the greater chance of a successful evasion when shot down over France.

In fact Petrie-Andrews and his crew had been rather fortunate to be rescued. It would not be strictly accurate to imply that ditching in the sea was a common occurrence but it was an additional hazard faced by crews returning in damaged aircraft and more especially from Berlin operations. Escape drills were regularly practised as were the 'ditching positions' to be taken in such an emergency. However, most crews felt 'it would not happen to us, and in any case we had more than enough other problems to worry about on an operation'. The accepted theory was that on ditching it was

---

Not a real Air/Sea Rescue – a practice exercise with a Supermarine Walrus.
(via T. Woods)

'tail in first then the nose'. Each crew member wore a yellow life jacket I, universally known as a *Mae West,* and each aircraft carried a yellow self-inflating dinghy, which carried emergency rations.

In August 1943 seventeen aircraft had ditched in the sea, six from the Peenemünde raid with a total loss of life. Nevertheless thirty airmen were rescued during the month, the majority by German vessels, and the crews ended up as prisoners of war. Out of the six aircraft that ditched after the Berlin operation on 23rd/24th only eight airmen survived. Three of these came from a Stirling of 90 Squadron; three sergeants survived for almost eight days in their dinghy before being rescued by the German *Kriegsmarine.* Somewhat tragically another Stirling crew of 196 Squadron from Witchford was sent out on the morning of the 24th to search for survivors in their dinghies; this was frequently done after large operations. The Stirling came down in the North Sea near the Danish coast and the seven-man crew were rather lucky to be rescued by a Danish fishing vessel, which had just happened to see the aircraft crash into the water. This was the first aircraft to be lost by the squadron since its move to Witchford. Many squadron records show missing aircraft as 'presumed lost over the sea', but the R.A.F.'s Air-Sea-Rescue Service with its fleet of fast motor-boats saved over 3,700 R.A.F. airmen, thus fully justifying its motto: 'The Sea Shall Not Have Them'.

In November 1943 a new PFF Mosquito squadron, No 627, was formed at Oakington under Wing Commander R.P. Elliott, D.S.O., D.F.C., who had previously commanded the Pathfinder Navigation Training Unit at Warboys, which gave a three-day course to new crews on PFF techniques. The squadron was not operational until the 24th when three crews left for Berlin. Also during the month one of 3 Group's premier squadrons, No 115, moved into Witchford. It had one of the finest operational records, having been a front-line squadron since October 1939, and during April 1941 its crews had undertaken the Service trials of *Gee.* Until it had changed to Lancaster IIs in May 1943, the squadron had been equipped with various Wellington marks and had carried out the most raids with them, the highest number of sorties and suffered the heaviest losses (ninety-eight) of any Wellington squadron. The first operation from Witchford was to Berlin on 26th/27th, when one crew failed to return. On 2nd/3rd December the crews had the distinction of dropping the first 8,000 lb bombs on the German capital.

On 3rd November, Harris wrote directly to Churchill and boldly claimed, 'We can wreck Berlin from end to end if the U.S.A.A.F. will come in on it. It

Lancaster III of 115 Squadron being loaded with an 8,000 lb bomb at Witchford.

will cost us 400-500 aircraft. It will cost Germany the war.' After recent very heavy losses on several daylight operations to German targets the U.S.A.A.F were loath to undertake any long-distance daylight operations until they were escorted by long-range fighters. In fact it was not until 6th March 1944 that their heavy bombers attacked Berlin for the first time. Thus Bomber Command was left fighting a lone battle over the German capital.

The Command's crews returned to 'The Big City' on 18th/19th November and over the next six weeks Berlin would be the target on another seven nights with the losses mounting alarmingly as the offensive was remorselessly pursued. On the first raid, once again only Lancaster crews were involved and the losses on this occasion were slight – seven aircraft – but four were from the PFF including an all-decorated crew of 156 Squadron captained by Wing Commander J. H. White, D.F.C., one of its most senior and experienced officers. Four nights later Halifaxes and Stirlings returned for the next Berlin raid and of the twenty-six crews that failed to return nine had left from Cambridgeshire airfields, including the Squadron Commander of No 83, Wing Commander R. Hilton, D.S.O.,

D.F.C. & Bar, who had only been in charge for three weeks.

Without question Cambridgeshire was now in the forefront of the Command's bombing offensive. Five out of fifty Stirlings were lost on this night and the decision was taken to withdraw the Stirling squadrons from German targets. Thus at a stroke of the pen Harris had 'lost' eleven squadrons and 3 Group was suddenly left with a minor role to play in the Command's strategy, at least until its squadrons re-equipped with Lancasters.

The Berlin operation on 2nd December, when forty crews (8.7%) failed to return, signalled the end of operations for one airman of 156 Squadron. I have previously remarked on the enormous contribution made by 'Halton' or 'Trenchard brats' to the R.A.F. during the Second World War. Flight Sergeant J. C. 'Charlie' Chapman, D.F.M., was just one of the hundreds of 'Halton brats' that served in Bomber Command and is very proud to be one. He had entered Halton as an apprentice in March 1940 at the age of sixteen. Two and a half years later he had qualified as a Flight Engineer on Lancasters and in January 1943 he was posted to his first operational squadron – No 156. At that time his flying experience amounted to about one hour as a passenger but that was soon to change most dramatically!

Charlie's first operation was to Lorient on 16th February 1943 at the tender age of nineteen years. His crew comprised two Canadians, two Englishmen, a Scot, an Australian and a Rhodesian, a not unusual make-up of a Bomber Command crew at this stage of the war. When they arrived safely back at Warboys, Charlie was asked by the Squadron Commander, Wing Commander Rivett-Carnac, what he thought of

Flight Sergeant J.C. 'Charlie' Chapman, D.F.M., in April 1944. (Kind permission Charlie Chapman)

his first operation. All he could reply was that he had been fascinated by the coloured tracers and flak. The C.O. told him to go and look at the tail plane and rear fuselage. It was riddled with bullet holes but fortunately no serious damage had been sustained – welcome to the air war!

Over the next ten months Charlie proceeded, night after night, to fly some of the most spectacular, punishing and costly operations mounted by the Command during that eventful year; his log book reads like a *Baedeker* of German cities and towns – the Battle of the Ruhr, four Hamburg raids, Peenemünde, no less than nine operations to the ultimate target, Berlin, as well as several trips to Italy. In November 1943 he was awarded an 'immediate' D.F.M., the citation stating that 'his example and devotion to duty made him very worthy of the immediate award'. His forty-seventh operation was successfully completed when his crew arrived safely back at Warboys in the early hours of 3rd December; his tour was over. All these operations had been flown during a time when the Command's and the PFF's losses had been steadily mounting. This amazing young man is an example of the thousands of youths who faced all the various dangers, time after time, and merely regarded it as their duty. Even at a distance of more than sixty years I find their courage breathtaking.

In January 1944 he found himself a highly experienced 'veteran' at the ripe old age of twenty years! He remained with the PFF, training new crews at the Pathfinder Navigational Training Unit, which had moved from Wyton to Warboys in April. After the war Charlie remained in the Service, operating in Transport Command and flying all over the world. His post-war service included the Berlin Air Lift (1948-9), the Korean War (1950-51) and the Malayan crisis (1951-2) – another fifty-seven operations completed! In September 1963 he retired from the R.A.F. after twenty-nine years' service with a total of 7,500 flying hours. Charlie Chapman is still very much alive, a most jovial and cheerful character and he is, without doubt, one of those countless 'unknown' heroes of Bomber Command and moreover an unsung airmen of the post-war years.

For those crews that had to soldier on, for twelve nights from 4th December 1943 there was not a single major operation mounted due to the full moon and weather conditions – a heaven-sent break. However, when they were back in action on the 16th/17th, the operation turned out to be a tragedy of some proportions, which became known as 'Black Thursday'. Few bomber squadrons managed to escape from at least one traumatic operation when things went drastically wrong and they suffered a heavy loss of aircraft and crews in a matter of a few hours. This happened to 97 Squadron on the 16th/17th when Berlin was once again the target. At the briefings most senior officers were convinced that the operation would be cancelled because of the strong probability of fog over the home bases later in the night. Nevertheless, it went ahead with the squadrons being despatched far earlier than usual in the hope that they would arrive back safely before the weather closed in.

Enemy action accounted for twenty-five Lancasters in total, one from 97 Squadron, but it was on their return that the problems started. Most of the bases in Cambridgeshire were closed in by low cloud. Eight crews out of nineteen did manage to land safely at Bourn, three landed at Graveley and another at Wyton. However, five crashed and another two were abandoned on orders. The squadron had lost eight aircraft (42%) with thirty-six airmen (including two Squadron Leaders) killed and another seven injured. This was the heaviest wartime loss for the squadron and a deep numbness pervaded Bourn for several weeks. It was a tragic start for the new Commander, Wing Commander C.M. Dunnicliffe, D.F.C., who had only taken over on the previous day.

Although 7 Squadron's losses were not quite so heavy, four of its Lancaster IIIs were shot down by night fighters. In fact the PFF lost seventeen aircraft, ninety-two airmen missing and another nineteen seriously injured. One of 156's missing crews was highly experienced; it was skippered by Flight Lieutenant C.O. Aubert, D.F.M., R.A.A.F., and the other seven members – mainly Australians – had four D.F.C.s and a D.F.M. between them. The PFF could not afford the steady loss of such experienced crews.

Two more Berlin raids brought to a close the most significant and memorable twelve months of the Command's entire bombing offensive. Such was its power and strength that despite all the losses suffered in the previous couple of months it was still able to despatch over seven hundred aircraft to Berlin on 29th/30th December.

Although much had been achieved during the year, the cost in aircraft and men had been very high; over 3,070 aircraft lost in action and accidents and 15,832 airmen killed with many thousands more taken prisoner and a countless number seriously injured. No less than 6,500 awards had been made to its airmen including four Victoria Crosses. Towards the end of the year as the relentless onslaught on Berlin continued, aircrew morale had been put under severe pressure but it did not weaken. Sadly, the early months of 1944 would place even greater strains on their courage and resolve.

Chapter 9

From the Skies Over Berlin to the Normandy Beaches

(JANUARY-6 JUNE 1944)

The first three months of 1944 tested the resolve of Bomber Command and its airmen to the utmost and beyond. During this period it suffered horrendous losses and that it managed to survive says much for the quality of its leadership right from upon high, down through Group, Station, Squadron and Flight Commanders to the Captains of individual crews. Its survival speaks volumes for the steely determination and will of its crews, flying night after night in atrocious weather conditions, facing both a resurgent *Luftwaffe* and continual heavy and concentrated flak. It also highlights the excellence and efficiency of its operational training programme that it was able to supply a sufficient number of trained crews to replace the enormous loss of airmen. Another important factor was the steady supply of new aircraft, especially Lancasters, which rolled off the production lines. Despite this quite grievous time, well before the year was out Bomber Command was at the zenith of its power, a massive strike force of heavy and light bombers.

On the first day of the New Year a new squadron was formed at Graveley

– No 692; it was equipped with Mosquito BIVs and was commanded by Wing Commander W. Guy Lockhart, D.S.O., D.F.C., Bar, Croix de Guerre. A remarkable and charismatic airman, Lockhart had been a fighter pilot, flown numerous secret missions in black Lysanders, and evaded capture when shot down over France by crossing to Spain before escaping from an internment camp. On return to the U.K. he completed a spell with Air Intelligence in the Air Ministry and now would lead a Mosquito squadron with great verve and daring until late March, when he moved to Oakington to take over command of 7 Squadron.

For the crews of the Lancaster squadrons the New Year opened with a flourish when on the first day over four hundred were despatched to Berlin, but because of severe weather conditions their departure was delayed until after midnight. The target was cloud covered and the sky marking was less than accurate. Twenty-eight crews (6.7%) were lost with the PFF suffering the heaviest loss – ten. This operation marked the start of a most traumatic time for the Pathfinders and, in particular, one squadron, No 156. On this night the squadron lost four aircraft with not a single survivor. Squadron Leader R.E. Fawcett, D.F.C., was on his third tour having completed sixty-nine operations and Squadron Leader R.G.F. Stewart was another experienced airman with forty-nine operations in his log book. Although 83 Squadron escaped lightly, its sole missing aircraft was shot down before

Mosquitos of 692 Squadron at Graveley; it formed part of the Light Night Striking Force. (via J. Adams)

reaching Berlin and was captained by its Commander, Wing Commander W. Abercromby, D.F.C., Bar.

The following night (2nd/3rd January) the crews might be forgiven for thinking that the operation would be 'scrubbed' as it had been snowing heavily. However, Harris ordered the operation to Berlin to go ahead and snow had to be quickly cleared from the runways for another midnight take-off. Over three hundred and sixty Lancasters and nine Halifaxes left and twenty-seven (7%) failed to return. Once again the PFF lost ten crews, half from 156 Squadron; in just two nights the squadron had lost seventy-one airmen in action, including Sergeant R.V. Hillman, who was only seventeen years old. To add to the squadron's woes one of its most senior and experienced leaders, Wing Commander L.C. 'Dixie' Dean, D.F.C., was moved to Wyton to take over the command of 83 Squadron.

After a welcome break due to the full moon period Brunswick was targeted for its first major raid of the war. On 14th/15th January almost five hundred Lancasters descended on the city, which is about one hundred miles west of Berlin. The operation proved to be a minor disaster for the Command and the PFF in particular, with thirty-eight aircraft (7.6%) shot down, most falling to night fighters; thirteen were Pathfinders and no less than five were from 156 Squadron – Warboys soon acquired the reputation as a 'chop station'.

In two weeks the PFF had lost forty-one aircraft and two hundred and seventy-three airmen. After this operation Air Vice-Marshal Bennett lamented that 'the loss of flight, squadron commanders and experienced crews was breaking the backbone of the Pathfinders'. Replacement crews

---

'Bon Voyage' – a final wave from some WAAFs along the runway as a Lancaster crew prepares to take off.

Messerschmitt 110: one of the several night fighters faced by the crews.

flooded in and airmen returning from leave found themselves as 'strangers in the Mess'. One airman serving with 156 remembered it as a time when it was not so much 'Here today and gone tomorrow but more here today and gone tonight'!

Five nights later (20th/21st) Berlin was the target, as it would be on another three January nights. There was a certain malaise evident with the crews, who were called upon time and time again to risk their lives over 'The Big City' and with such heavy losses could see little chance of their survival. Interspersed between these Berlin raids was a most costly operation to Magdeburg on 21st/22nd when fifty-seven aircraft were lost, thirty-five of them Halifaxes at a loss rate of 15.6%. This proved to be the highest casualty rate on a single night so far. It was thought that over three-quarters had fallen to night fighters. In fact during January 1944 the Command lost more aircraft and crews than in any other month of the war. It was clear that Bomber Command was losing out to the *Luftwaffe* in the battle of the night skies.

For the first fourteen nights of February not a single major bombing operation was mounted because of the moon period. This unusually long break in operations was further extended by the weather, with heavy snow falling from the 13th to the 15th. After the rigours and traumas of the previous month, there was a discernible easing of tension in the crews, who

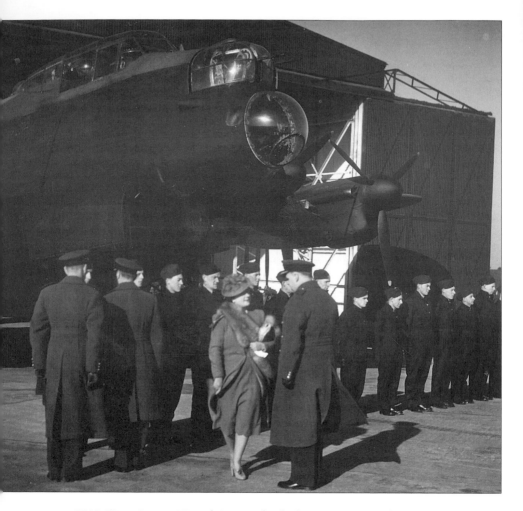

H.M. King George VI and Queen Elizabeth inspect crews of 156 Squadron at Warboys, February 1944.

had precious time to relax, recover and moreover to sleep soundly. Their Majesties King George IV and Queen Elizabeth took the opportunity to visit some bomber stations. On the 10th they were at Graveley, Gransden Lodge and Warboys. It was said that H.M. The King took a particular interest in the Pathfinders and was well aware of the crucial role they were playing in the air offensive. The visits were informal affairs with the officers and airmen that were on parade wearing normal working battledress. The visits were greatly appreciated by the crews; they felt that he was 'their' King, as 'he had once served in the R.A.F.'.

Five days later these very airmen were somewhat shocked to discover at their briefings that 'the red ribbon disclosed yet another long haul to Berlin', the seventh time in a matter of a month and a half. Over eight hundred and ninety aircraft took part, the largest number sent to Berlin and the tonnage of bombs was also a record – 2,642. Forty-three crews (4.8%) failed to return, seven from the PFF of which four came from 7 Squadron; two highly decorated Squadron Leaders – J.A. Hagman, D.S.O., D.F.C., R.N.Z.A.F., and R.D. Campling, D.S.O., D.F.C., along with Wing Commander J.B. Tatnell, O.B.E., and a number of other experienced and decorated airmen were lost. Along with 156 Squadron, No 7 was suffering heavy losses of senior crews; Squadron Leader Hagman was aged forty years, well over the age associated with the Command's captains.

Back in November 1943 it had been agreed that a combined Allied bombing offensive would be directed against the German aircraft industry and the production of ball bearings. The proposed offensive code-named *Argument* was planned to take place early in 1944 when a favourable spell of weather was forecast. This happened on 19th February and on that evening the Command opened *Argument*, later popularly known as 'The Big Week', with a heavy raid directed at Leipzig. It was an unhappy night for the Command, the seventy-eight aircraft lost (9.5%) surpassing the losses over Magdeburg less than a month earlier. The PFF squadrons lost ten crews including eight experienced Squadron Leaders. On this night it was the turn of 35 Squadron to bear the brunt, four of its Halifaxes failed to return to Graveley including the legendary Julian Slade. In fact thirty-four Halifaxes went missing on the night, almost 15%, and as a result the older Halifax marks were permanently removed from German targets.

'The Big Week' continued with operations to Stuttgart, Schweinfurt and finally Augsburg on the 25th/26th, which was the most successful because of the clear skies over the target and accurate marking. This raid became quite controversial because the fine old centre of Augsburg was completely destroyed, with the German propaganda machine calling it 'an extreme example of terror bombing'. During the week over 2,700 crews had been in action and one hundred and forty-five (5.2%) were missing. The PFF might be said to have escaped fairly lightly with twenty crews lost in action though seven of these belonged to 156 Squadron, their ill-luck continuing to dog them. One of the crews was captained by Wing Commander E. F. Porter, who was flying his sixteenth operation. He was a fairly rare breed of Command airman, having joined the Service in the late 1920s; there were not that many pre-war regular airmen of such seniority still flying operationally. As a comparison, the American Eighth Air Force flew over 3,000 sorties during the week and lost one hundred and fifty-eight aircraft (4.7%). Germany was now suffering 'round the clock' bombing with a vengeance.

There was at least one other pre-war regular officer flying with the PFF, the exceptional Wing Commander G.H. 'Geoff' Womersley, D.S.O., Bar, D.F.C., MiD. He had joined the R.A.F. in 1936 and became a bomber pilot

Wing Commander G.H. 'Geoff' Womersley, D.S.O., Bar, D.F.C., MiD – one of the 'living legends' of Bomber Command. (R.A.F Museum)

with 102 Squadron, flying the open-cockpit Handley Page Heyfords. As a Pilot Officer he completed his first operational tour in July 1940 as captain of a Whitley and had already successfully evaded capture after being shot down over France. After a spell as a flying training instructor, he returned to operations as a Squadron Leader flying Wellingtons with 75 (NZ) Squadron. With the formation of the PFF in August 1942 he volunteered for the Pathfinders and was readily accepted, joining 156 Squadron in that month. Geoff was awarded the D.S.O. in January 1943, followed by his D.F.C. in April. After completing his second tour, he was posted to the PFF staff before being given the command of 139 Mosquito Squadron in February 1944. He remained with the squadron at Upwood until October and was later given the command of Gransden Lodge at the rank of Group Captain. It is interesting to note that Geoff considered the Lancaster 'the best plane he ever flew'. After the war he joined his ex-boss Donald Bennett on his South American Airways, which later amalgamated with B.O.A.C., where he remained as a Captain until retiring in 1968. A consummate airman and a modest and charming gentleman; at the time of writing Geoff is alive and well – a true living legend of Bomber Command.

With the removal of Stirlings from German targets, the 'bread and butter' missions for their crews were 'gardening', bombing the V-1 ('flying bomb') sites in northern France, and dropping supplies to resistance units mainly in France. Thus 75 (NZ) Squadron at Mepal was able to survive the early months of 1944 with relatively few casualties. It had been decided to equip the squadron with Lancasters but it proved to be a slow and protracted business as most of the production was reserved to provide replacements for the existing Lancaster squadrons, which had suffered heavy losses in the Berlin operations.

Towards the end of 1943 intelligence had revealed that a number of 'construction sites' were being prepared in the Pas de Calais, thought to be for the assembly, storage and launching of 'unmanned bombs'. Indeed so serious was the threat that the Command, along with the U.S.A.A.F., devoted a large amount of their resources to these 'construction sites', which was exactly what the crews were told they were. The operations became known as 'Crossbow' or 'Noball' targets, although quite soon rumours persisted that the sites were 'for rockets' and the Pas de Calais quickly became known as 'the rocket coast'. From 13th June the attacks on these sites intensified when the first V-1s fell on south-east England.

During February 1944 many of the PFF Mosquitos were modified to accommodate a 4,000 lb High Capacity bomb or 'Cookie'. The extra weight altered the aircraft's centre of gravity and induced a certain instability; as one pilot recalled, 'they called for delicate handling and gentle persuasion rather like a WAAF'! The first 'Cookie' was dropped on Düsseldorf on 23rd/24th from a height of 25,000 ft by crews of 692 Squadron and the first Mosquito 'Cookies' fell on Berlin on 13th/14th April. Because of the increased weight two additional drop tanks were necessary for the Berlin operations but they made the trip in less than half the time of Lancasters. Bennett's Light Night Striking Force dropped over 1,400 'Cookies' on the German capital during the course of the war.

With the Allied invasion, Operation *Overlord*, only months away, the

Allied Chiefs of Staff decided that it was time to activate the Transportation Plan, which had been designed to attack important rail centres and junctions, marshalling yards and rolling stock in northern France and Belgium in an attempt to prevent troop reinforcements and supplies being sent forward to Normandy after the invasion. The Plan had been hotly debated, partly on account of the high risk to the civilian population but also because Harris and his American counterpart considered that their heavy bombers would be better deployed over German industrial targets. Harris also had some reservations about his Force's ability to mark and bomb accurately such small and precise targets. Nevertheless the Plan was approved and the Command was allocated thirty-seven targets. The first, Trappes marshalling yards in France, was attacked on 6th/7th March. These short-range operations were ideal for Stirlings, and the three remaining squadrons – 75, 90 and 149 – were frequently engaged in such raids before being joined by the heavy squadrons, mainly from April onwards. Well over half of the Command's rail targets had been destroyed by D-Day.

During the whole of March 1944 the Command mounted only six major

A Mosquito being loaded with a 4,000 lb 'Cookie' bomb. (via T. Murphy)

*The Berlin War Cemetery: a peaceful scene some fifty years after
'The Battle of Berlin'. (via B. Jones)*

operations but the last two proved to be disasters of horrific proportions. Two German cities, Stuttgart and Frankfurt, suffered two heavy raids; the second to Frankfurt on 22nd/23rd March was one of devastating accuracy, which German officials described as 'the worst and most fateful blow of the war...which simply ended the existence of Frankfurt that had been built up since the Middle Ages'. Compared with the losses the Command had sustained in the previous two months, the cost of these four operations might be considered minimal – average 2.4%. But such statistics were of little comfort to those squadrons that had lost crews. On the first Stuttgart operation on 15th/16th, 35 Squadron lost its first Lancaster III in action – one of the air gunners, Sergeant A.H. Neller, was one of the oldest operational airmen at forty-one years old. On the same night 97 Squadron also had one crew missing, where every single member was decorated; this was not unique but certainly it was highly unusual. On the second Frankfurt operation, 7 Squadron lost two aircraft, one captained by its Commander, Group Captain K.J. Rampling, D.S.O., D.F.C.; the fates were no respecter of age, seniority, rank or indeed experience.

The final operation in 'The Battle of Berlin' was mounted on 24th/25th, although the eight hundred and eleven crews detailed for the raid were unaware that it was likely to be the last time they would go to 'The Big City'. This operation became known as 'the night of the strong winds' when powerful and ferocious northerly winds scattered the force, especially on the homeward flight. It was the first time that the scientific world became aware of 'jet streams' in the upper atmosphere. Seventy-two crews (9.1%) failed to return, fifty of them believed to have been shot down by enemy flak. This particular Battle had been waged relentlessly with great determination but at a very high cost – almost 11,000 sorties flown for the loss of six hundred and twenty aircraft, equivalent to twenty-four squadrons and most of them Lancasters. Over 3,800 airmen were missing in action; of these about 80% were killed and the majority are buried in the Berlin War Cemetery.

The *Official History* was perhaps a little harsh on Air Chief Marshal Harris: 'the expectations of the C-in-C had not been fulfilled and by that standard the Battle of Berlin had been a failure...Moreover in the operational sense, the Battle was more than a failure. It was a defeat.' Nevertheless it had caused a massive diversion of German resources into defence and thus made a valuable contribution to the war being waged on the Eastern Front and ultimately the Allied invasion of Europe. However, for the crews, such strategic nuances were of little or no concern, all agreed that their trips to 'The Big City' were the most traumatic and fearsome of their tours – 'the worst weather...the coldest conditions...the heaviest flak...the most number of searchlights and the greatest fighter opposition'. One bomb aimer of 156 Squadron recalled that 'lying in the nose of a Lancaster on a visual bomb run over Berlin was probably the most frightening experience of my lifetime...every second I expected to be blown to pieces. I sweated with fear, and the perspiration seemed to freeze on my body'.

After the mayhem of the final Berlin raid, on the following day over seven hundred crews entered their briefing rooms to be told that Essen was to be 'the target for tonight', though in truth they were pleased that it was not going to be Berlin again and there were precious few remaining crews that could remember those costly Essen missions back in the Battle of the Ruhr. On this night the change to a Ruhr target caught the German fighter controllers on the wrong foot and only nine aircraft failed to return, the lowest rate so far sustained over Essen, and not a single PFF aircraft was lost – a unique occurrence.

Any fleeting hopes that the Essen operation had marked 'the turning of the

A Lancaster crew waits for their aircraft to be prepared for action. (via J. Adams)

tide' in the battle with the *Luftwaffe*'s night fighters were quickly, ruthlessly and cruelly dispelled just four nights later. On 30th March Nuremberg in southern Germany was selected as the target for seven hundred and ninety-five crews from fifty squadrons. The city was considered the administrative heart of the German aircraft industry as well as being a very special place for the Nazi party: 'the Holy City of the evil Nazi creed', as one Station Commander described it at his briefing.

It was an undoubted risk to send such a large force to this distant target so late in the moon period, although there had been a weather forecast of the presence of high cloud on the outward flight, which proved to be incorrect. The bomber stream, some thirty-eight miles long, flew in bright moonlight making distinctive white contrails in the cold night sky. One survivor, in his later years, maintained, 'Even now, when I see a bright moon, I think of it as a Nuremberg moon.' By one of those cruel twists of fate the German fighter controllers had assembled their night fighters over two radio beacons – *Ida* to the south-east of Aachen and *Otto* to the north of Frankfurt – almost precisely on the bombers' planned outward route.

Returning from Nuremberg on 31st March 1944,
this Lancaster II of No 115 Squadron, piloted by
Flight Sergeant T.W.H. Fogarty, D.F.M., crash-landed
to the south of Stuttgart. (via A.R. Bryant)

Actually seven hundred and eighty crews left for Nuremberg on that fateful night, and of these fifty-two (6.9%) returned early for a variety of reasons but mainly engine and oxygen failures. These 'early returns' were something of a vexed issue and those returning crews faced a searching interview with their Station or Squadron Commander; an 'early return' did not count as an operational sortie unless the crew claimed that they had dropped their bombs on an enemy target. The percentage of 'early returns' on this night was about average. Thus seven hundred and thirty crews flew on through the bright moonlight and no less than eighty-two were shot down before reaching their target. As one airman later said, 'I still have nightmares about seeing so many Lancasters going down in flames.'

For about an hour and a half the crews were engaged in a ceaseless battle with well over two hundred night fighters all the way to Nuremberg. Then over the target heavy cloud and strong crosswinds prevented accurate marking and bombing and the damage was minimal; also about one sixth of the crews bombed Schweinfurt, some fifty miles to the north-east, in error. Mercifully the return trip was much easier as many of the fighters had landed to re-fuel; nevertheless ninety-five aircraft had been lost in action and another ten crashed on return to the United Kingdom. This proved to be the highest loss ever suffered by Bomber Command on one night – over 14%. Some seven hundred and ten airmen were missing, of whom one hundred and fifty were taken prisoner, the largest haul of the war. Over five hundred and forty airmen had been killed, more lost in a single night than Fighter Command's *total* losses during the Battle of Britain.

Quite remarkably nine squadrons escaped intact and the PFF, on this occasion, incurred fairly light casualties, twelve in total, four of which came from the unfortunate 156 Squadron – its losses during the first three months amounted to a half of its total losses for 1944. Early in the month the squadron had moved from Warboys to Upwood, but the new station had not brought a change in their fortunes. Another Cambridgeshire squadron, 514 at Waterbeach, lost six Lancasters out of nineteen (35%). Half of the missing crews had completed ten or less operations and eight were on their first operation; clearly the more experienced a crew was the greater chance of their survival. Although there were still a number of crews that were on their second operational tours, including Flight Lieutenant D.H. Rowlands, D.F.C., of 97 Squadron and his crew, one of which, Flight Lieutenant R.A.D. Trevor-Roper, D.F.C., D.F.M., had been Guy Gibson's rear gunner on the epic Dams raid back in May 1943.

The Nuremberg raid resulted in one posthumous Victoria Cross to Pilot Officer Cyril J. Burton, a Halifax pilot of 578 Squadron, for 'gallantry in the face of almost impossible odds'. There were countless other acts of heroism. Flight Sergeant T.W.H. Fogarty, D.F.M., of 115 Squadron at Witchford, for instance, ordered his crew to bale out of their badly damaged Lancaster and when the Flight Engineer could not locate his parachute, Fogarty unselfishly handed him his own. Left alone, Fogarty managed to crash-land the stricken aircraft near Stuttgart and he escaped with minor injuries, joining the rest of his crew as a prisoner of war. Like 156 Squadron, 115 had suffered heavy losses in the early months of 1944, almost thirty aircraft missing, which was then the highest casualty rate in the Command. In just one week the Command had lost one hundred and seventy aircraft and crews in action.

The PFF techniques and performance were being seriously questioned within the Service, and more especially after the ill-fated Berlin operations,

The tension still shows as this Lancaster crew of No 115 Squadron arrives safely back at Witchford in early 1944. (via W.M. Smith)

although the *Luftwaffe* had no doubts about its efficacy and the crews' expertise. A German Staff paper was circulated in March:

> The operational tactics of the Pathfinders have been under constant development ever since the earliest days, and even now cannot be considered firmly established or completed...The realisation of these aims was made possible by the conscientious work of the Pathfinder group and by the high training standing (especially regarding navigation) of the crews.

This was high praise indeed from the enemy! Nevertheless the Commander of 5 Group, Air Vice-Marshal the Hon R.A. Cochrane, who had been the Pathfinders' sternest critic, had been experimenting with a different kind of marking – the low-level identification of targets.

In April Air Chief Marshal Harris was convinced of the soundness of his theories and he allowed 5 Group to become an almost independent force responsible for its own marking. Despite Bennett's protests two Lancaster squadrons – 83 and 97 – along with a Mosquito squadron – 627 – were transferred to 5 Group. However, his Group had acquired a new Lancaster squadron, No 582, which was formed at Little Staughton, an airfield that had been given up by the U.S.A.A.F.; it was sited in Bedfordshire but was bordered on three sides by the Cambridgeshire county boundary. Also the two *Oboe* Mosquito squadrons – 105 and 109 – moved closer to the Pathfinders headquarters at Huntingdon. No 105 moved into Bourn, which was rather appropriate as the new Station Commander or 'Station Master' there was Group Captain H.E. Bufton D.S.O., D.F.C., A.F.C., who had pioneered the use of *Oboe* with 109 Squadron; his old squadron arrived at Little Staughton during April.

The operations during the first three months of the year had produced a staggering rate of attrition, so it was perhaps fortunate that for the next two months or so the crews would be mainly engaged in attacking those targets selected as a prelude to D-Day – the French railway system and gun batteries in the Pas de Calais as part of the grand deception plan to convince the enemy that the imminent invasion would take place there. There was a break from operations until 9th April when railway targets in northern France were bombed. The Master and Deputy Bomber technique was invariably used and because these operations were conducted at low-level for greater accuracy they proved to be highly dangerous for those airmen chosen for these important tasks, as the loss of a number of experienced pilots and crews confirmed.

The control of Bomber Command, along with the American Eighth Air Force, passed to General Dwight Eisenhower, the Supreme Allied Commander in Europe, on 14th April 1944 and it would remain so until mid-September; although the control was effectively in the hands of his Deputy, Air Chief Marshal Sir Arthur W. Tedder. As Air Chief Marshal Harris later recalled: 'The

Railway targets in northern France were frequently bombed during April and May 1944.
(via A.R. Bryant)

comparatively brief period was absolutely the only time during the whole of my command when I was able to proceed with a campaign without being harassed by confused and conflicting directives.' Nevertheless when other priorities allowed, Harris did target a number of German cities during April, such as Cologne, Düsseldorf, Essen, Munich, Schweinfurt and Friedrichshafen on 27th/28th.

Friedrichshafen could be considered a legitimate target in the light of the coming invasion, as there were several factories manufacturing engines and gearboxes for tanks. It was situated in the far south of Germany on the shores of Lake Constance. The raid was conducted in bright moonlight and entailed a long flight, which must have been a calculated risk considering the Nuremberg losses of less than a month earlier. It was rated as 'an outstandingly successful attack' with excellent PFF marking; eighteen Lancasters (5.6%) were lost. Amongst the missing crews were two PFF Squadron Commanders – Group Captain E.C. Eaton, D.F.C., of 156 and Wing Commander W.G. Lockhart, D.S.O., D.F.C., of 7 Squadron. Bennett said of Lockhart, 'I never, throughout the entire war met anybody so fanatically courageous and "press on" at all times and in all circumstances. Virtually nothing would stop him...his determination passed all bounds.'

Squadron Commanders were expected to fly operationally at least once a month but most flew far more frequently. During April and May six were killed in action, four whilst leading PFF squadrons. As one airman remarked, 'The grim reaper has no respect for rank.' On 19th/20th May, 7 Squadron lost its third Commander in a matter of months. Wing Commander J. Fraser Barron, D.S.O., Bar, D.F.C., Bar, a brilliant young New Zealand pilot, had already completed two tours, although he was only twenty-three years old. Barron was on his seventy-ninth operation when, acting as Master Bomber over the railway yards at Le Mans, his Lancaster collided over the target with that of the Deputy Master, Squadron Leader J.M. Dennis, D.S.O., D.F.C.; it was a staggering blow for the squadron and the PFF to lose such outstanding airmen and their experienced crews.

On the night before D-Day (6th June 1944) Bomber Command flew over 1,200 sorties and dropped at least 5,000 tons of bombs on the batteries behind the Normandy beaches. The total number of sorties was a new record, as was the bomb tonnage, and just eight aircraft (0.7%) were lost. Since 1st April the crews had been in action on fifty-seven nights for the loss of five hundred and twenty-five aircraft (2.2%), a most encouraging and marked reduction to the rate that had been sustained earlier in the year. With the Allied armies safely landed on the Normandy beaches, surely the end of the war was now in sight?

'Tail-end Charlie' – a Lancaster rear gunner.
(via W.M. Smith)

Chapter 10

Back to Germany By Day and By Night

(June-December 1944)

With the Allied armies safely landed in Normandy, the Command's crews were frequently called upon to provide battle support, bombing German troop positions, gun batteries, ammunition and oil dumps as well as rail and road communications behind the enemy lines. Then, when the first flying-bomb landed on English soil on 13th June 1944, for the next two and a half months they were frequently engaged in bombing V1 flying-bomb sites and stores. However, the German synthetic oil industry remained the main strategic priority for both Bomber Command and the American Eighth Air Force.

Perhaps the most significant feature of the Command's offensive until the end of the year was its increasing strength and power. Its number of front-line aircraft increased by 50% during the year, mostly in the second half, and the number of operations it mounted by day doubled its effectiveness. One very welcome aspect was the reduction of the overall loss rate from 3.6% earlier in the year to 1.2% by the end of the year. This meant that the crews' chances of surviving an operational tour had been greatly enhanced.

But such bare statistics, however encouraging they were to 'the powers that be' at Command headquarters, hid the fact that on some operations the rate of loss was far higher and a number of squadrons suffered quite heavily on a single operation. In this respect the PFF escaped relatively lightly; two PFF squadrons, 7 and 156, that had previously suffered harshly, managed to get through July with just one crew of 156 Squadron missing in action, although it was a most experienced crew, captained by Squadron Leader G.C. Davies, D.S.O., and where the other seven members were all officers (still quite a rarity), four of them decorated with D.F.C.s.

The Pathfinder Force did lose a supreme bomber captain during July – Wing Commander Alec P. Cranswick, D.S.O., D.F.C., of 35 Squadron. On 4th/5th July the marshalling yards at Villeneuve St Georges to the south of Paris were the target and because of heavy cloud the crews were forced to bomb from 4/5,000 ft to ensure greater accuracy. The heavy flak accounted for eleven Lancasters, two from 35 Squadron, one of which was piloted by Wing Commander Cranswick; it received a direct hit, burst into flames and before the crew could bale out the aircraft broke up. Only the wireless operator, Flight Sergeant W.R. Horner, survived, blown out by the power of the explosion.

Cranswick had started his operational service in June 1940 with 214 Squadron flying Wellingtons and by October 1943, whilst serving with 35 Squadron, he had completed three operational tours. After a spell at PFF headquarters he returned to the squadron in April 1944 to commence his fourth tour. When he was killed he was only twenty-four years old and it was thought that he had completed one hundred and seven missions, although Bennett's book, *Pathfinder*, claims that the correct figure was one hundred and forty-three. Such was Bennett's esteem for this

Wing Commander Alec P. Cranswick, D.S.O., D.F.C., of 35 Squadron: 'simply a quiet honest Englishman.'.

exceptional airman that he dedicated his book to Cranswick and described him as 'not a flamboyant roistering character but simply a quiet honest Englishman... so simply courageous and so selfless in his sacrifice'; words that could equally apply to so many thousands of Bomber Command airmen.

Besides Alec Cranswick, two other legendary pilots of Bomber Command bowed out of operations during this period of the war. Wing Commander Leonard Cheshire, D.S.O., 2 Bars, D.F.C., the Commander of 617 Squadron, was ordered to rest after leading an operation to the Mimoyecques flying-bomb site on 6th July. He had completed four tours and flown one hundred operations; two months later he was awarded the Victoria Cross for 'a record second to none in Bomber Command'. Wing Commander Guy Gibson, V.C.,

Wing Commander Keith 'Slim' Somerville, D.S.O., D.F.C., A.F.C., took over No 105 Squadron in September 1944.

D.S.O., Bar, D.F.C., Bar, was allowed to leave his desk job for just one more operation on 19th/20th September; he flew a Mosquito of 627 Squadron as the Master Bomber on a raid to Rheydt and Mönchengladbach. On the return flight Gibson's Mosquito inexplicably crashed in Holland and he and his navigator, Squadron Leader J.B. Warwick, D.F.C., were killed in the explosion.

With the departure of such famous airmen, precious links were being severed with the nascent and struggling Command of the early war years. Although in September one such 'veteran' (although he was only twenty-four years old!) arrived at Bourn to take over the command of 105 Squadron. Wing Commander Keith 'Slim' Somerville, D.S.O., D.F.C., A.F.C., was a pre-war officer, who had joined the R.A.F. in 1938. He completed his first tour of thirty-five operations flying Whitleys with No 10 Squadron. One of the four pilots selected to develop *Oboe*, he returned to operations flying Mosquitos and went on the first *Oboe* raid in December 1942, and then in July 1944 he also flew the first *Oboe*-equipped Lancaster operation. In

ND917 of 'C' Flight, 75 (NZ) Squadron, was the first Lancaster to land on an airstrip in France – 30th June 1944.

March 1945 he was promoted to Group Captain at the age of twenty-five and was also awarded the D.S.O. for 'his example of coolness and courage in the face of the fiercest enemy fire'. He was an exceptional pilot, who led his crews by example, and by the end of the war he had completed no less than one hundred and seventeen operations. Somerville left the R.A.F. in 1946 and died in October 2004 at the age of eighty-four years.

Some squadrons were still suffering disastrous operations and one befell 75 (NZ) Squadron on 20th/21st July when the Scholver-Buer synthetic-oil refinery at Homberg was the target for one hundred and forty-seven Lancasters; the plant was thought to provide the *Luftwaffe* with about 6,000 tons of aviation fuel daily. Although severe damage was inflicted, with the production of valuable oil greatly reduced, it proved to be a costly operation as night fighters shot down most of the missing twenty Lancasters (13.6%). Seven of these came from 75 (NZ) Squadron (28%) with forty-nine airmen missing in action, and only eight survived. They were mostly

New Zealanders; amongst those killed was an eighteen year old air gunner, Sergeant J.L. Stephenson, whereas another Sergeant, J. Armstrong, was aged forty years, one of the oldest airmen killed in 1944. Another Cambridgeshire squadron, 514 lost four crews on the same operation. And yet just three weeks earlier (30th June) 75 (NZ) Squadron had created a little bit of R.A.F. history when one of its Lancasters, ND917, piloted by Squadron Leader N. A. Williamson, D.F.C., R.N.Z.A.F., made an emergency landing on a Normandy air-strip, the first R.A.F. heavy bomber to do so.

Although the reins of Bomber Command were not returned to Air Chief Marshal Harris until 14th September, he managed to take his Force back to Germany, the port of Kiel, on 23rd/24th July 1944, the first time for two months that the crews had been briefed for a German city. The following night Stuttgart was bombed as it would be on two other nights in quick succession. They caused the heaviest damage that Stuttgart suffered in the whole of the war. The third operation conducted on 28th/29th in bright moonlight, was the most costly with thirty-nine Lancasters (7.9%) being shot down, mainly by night fighters whilst over France on the outward flight, clearly showing that the *Luftwaffe* was not yet a spent force. Although the PFF squadrons survived the nightly ordeals relatively intact, 75 (NZ) Squadron lost four crews; it was experiencing a costly month. No 514 Squadron at Waterbeach lost three crews in the three operations, although six of one eight-man crew all managed to successfully evade capture when their Lancaster crashed at Châtendun about eighty miles south-west of Paris.

The majority of the operations conducted by day were to French railway targets and V-1 flying-bomb sites but on 27th August the Command launched a daylight raid on a German city for the first time in over three years. Once again a synthetic-oil refinery at Homberg was the target and the two hundred and forty bombers were escorted by nine squadrons of Spitfires; although heavy flak was encountered over the target, not a single aircraft was lost – 'a blessed relief'! During the following months the Command's daylight operations increased in size and severity with many German targets suffering raids by day and by night. At the end of the year daylight operations accounted for 40% of the Command's total operations.

On 28th August 1944 twelve V-1 flying-bomb sites were bombed by day with considerable success and only a single Lancaster was lost. This operation proved to be the last time these sites were attacked as within a few days the Allied ground forces captured most of them. Over the next few months the crews were called upon on several occasions to support the advancing Allied armies, notably at Arnhem and the German counter-offensive in the Ardennes in late December.

In relating the story of Bomber Command and its crews, the immense contribution made by the Mosquito crews can be somewhat overlooked. This is possibly due to their very low loss rate and the fact that they comprised just two airmen – pilot and navigator – compared with the seven-man Lancaster crew. It is from this period until the final day of the European war that can be considered their greatest hour. By the end of the year there were ten Mosquito squadrons in the main force, nine of which were serving in the PFF, and all except one, No 608, were operating from Cambridgeshire airfields.

Besides their vital role of *Oboe* marking, the 'Mossie' crews were engaged on a variety of tasks – dropping flares and target indicators, making 'diversionary' raids, dropping 'window' ahead of the main force by day

---

Over five months some 3,000 tons of bombs were dropped on the large V-1 flying-bomb site and stores at Siracourt in the Pas de Calais.

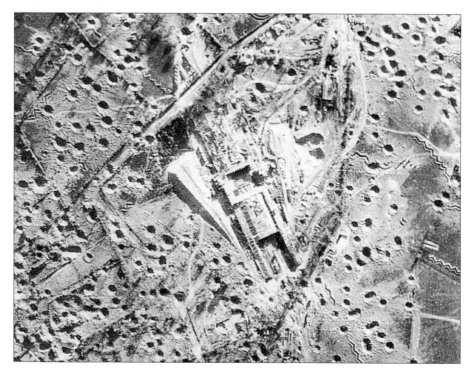

Mosquito XX (KB929) of No 139 Squadron; it was shot down by a night fighter on 24th/25th June 1944 during a Berlin operation. Flight Lieutenant W.W. Boylson, D.F.C., Bar, and Squadron Leader G.H. Wilson, D.S.O., D.F.C., were both killed.

and night and mainly roaming around Germany nightly bombing cities and towns, most notably Berlin. The Mosquitos were frequently in action on nights when the heavy bomber squadrons were rested, indeed on no less than sixty-five nights from D-Day to the end of the year. During this period one hundred and forty-five PFF Mosquitos were lost with seventy-eight airmen missing, of which number sixty-one were killed.

The majority of these 'Mossie' crews were highly experienced and decorated airmen; many had already completed at least one tour with a heavy bomber squadron. Sadly a number lost their lives during this time. For instance, the highly experienced 139 Squadron crew – Flight Lieutenant W.W. Boylson, D.F.C., Bar, and Squadron Leader G.H. Wilson, D.S.O., D.F.C., – failed to return from Berlin on 24th/25th June. Then on 7th July Squadron Leader W. 'Bill' Blessing, D.S.O., D.F.C., R.A.A.F., of 105 Squadron was killed over Caen; his Mosquito experience dated back to late 1942 and he was one of the most experienced Mosquito pilots in the Command. Three nights later (10th/11th) Wing Commander S.D. Watts, D.S.O., D.F.C., and Pilot Officer A.A. Matheson, D.F.M., both New Zealanders of 571 Squadron, were shot down over Berlin. The Berlin defences claimed another experienced pilot, Squadron Leader T.E. Dodwell, D.F.C., Bar, also of 571 Squadron. During the autumn and the winter the grim toll continued.

Although the losses sustained by the PFF Mosquito squadrons were amazingly low and can even be considered infinitesimal when compared with the heavy bomber squadrons – one hundred in total or 0.4% – such figures belie the ultimate sacrifice of these brave and intrepid Mosquito men. And yet the only *Oboe* Mosquito pilot to be awarded the Victoria Cross – Squadron Leader R.A.M. Palmer of 109 Squadron – was actually captaining a Lancaster at the time of his award!

In addition to the eight PFF Mosquito squadrons operating from Cambridgeshire airfields, there were also nine Lancaster squadrons, five with the PFF and four serving in the renascent No 3 Group, which, in the months ahead, would be given a new and important role to play in the Command's strategic offensive.

On 13th October 1944 Harris received a directive to activate Operation *Hurricane*, which was 'to demonstrate to the enemy in Germany generally the overwhelming superiority of the Allied Air Forces...the intention is to apply within the shortest practical period the maximum effort of the Royal Air Force and the VIIIth U.S. Bomber Command against objectives in the densely populated Ruhr.'

This directive seemed to be 'tailor-made' for Air Chief Marshal Harris and the following day he launched a devastating attack on Duisburg, followed by a night operation to both Duisburg and Brunswick. The night operation was divided into two forces, two hours apart. In a matter of twenty-four hours almost 2,600 crews took part, dropping over 10,000 tons of bombs; these records would not be exceeded again in the war. It was an awesome and terrifying demonstration of the power of Bomber Command, all undertaken at a relatively small cost – twenty-four aircraft lost, a mere 0.9%. During the same period the American Eighth Air Force attacked railway yards in Cologne but not with the same power.

From now until the end of the year the Command seemed to be running out of targets. Much of the Ruhr lay in ruins and although some 'favourites' – Essen, Cologne, Düsseldorf...*et al* – were attacked, a number of German cities and towns were bombed for the first time, although the main priorities remained synthetic-oil refineries and plants along with the German transportation system prior to the steady advance of the Allied armies. One city, Darmstadt, about twenty-five miles south of Frankfurt, suffered very heavy damage and great loss of life on 11th/12th September; the German authorities claimed it as an extreme example of R.A.F. 'terror bombing'. The outstandingly accurate raid had been made by a relatively small force of two hundred and forty Lancasters and Mosquitos; it presaged similar heavy attacks on other German towns in the coming months. This operation on Darmstadt, along with the Command's attacks on Hamburg and Dresden, has been used in the post-war years to criticise the morality of the Command's policy of 'area bombing'.

During October 1944 many of 3 Group's Lancasters were equipped with *G-H*, the blind-bombing aid, which enabled the force to bomb in almost any weather conditions. It employed *Gee* in conjunction with an airborne transmitter/receiver and two ground stations as beacons. Air Vice-Marshal R. Harrison, A.O.C. of 3 Group, had been given a relatively free hand with his Lancaster squadrons; by the end of the year he had ten, four of which – 75 (NZ), 115, 195 and 514 – were based at Cambridgeshire airfields. The main feature of the *G-H* operations was that they comprised small forces of Lancasters operating mainly by day and escorted by fighters which bombed accurately on *G-H* leaders, with a remarkably low loss rate of

Another operation successfully completed. One of the 126 Lancaster crews to return safely from Duisburg on 1st December 1944. (via R. Matthews)

aircraft. The *G-H* force's first operation was to Bonn on 18th October, a city that had not been previously bombed and which was probably selected to show the efficacy of *G-H*. The attack was a complete and utter success, very heavy damage was inflicted and only one of the one hundred and twenty-eight Lancasters was lost, which happened to come from 115 Squadron at Witchford.

From that date until the end of the year 3 Group mounted thirty-two operations, all but three of them by day, over 4,100 sorties for the loss of forty-five Lancasters (1%). Because *G-H* had a restricted range the 3 Group crews were mainly engaged in bombing oil targets in and around the Ruhr as well as a variety of railway targets. Although such losses were quite minimal in the grand scale of things, there were a few *G-H* operations when the Cambridgeshire squadrons suffered. On 30th November when the *G-H* force bombed the Meerbeck oil plant at Homberg and five Lancasters failed to return, three of the crews were of 75 (NZ) Squadron; one crew was very experienced with four of its members being over thirty years old, a quite rare occurrence at this time of the war. On 12th December when the steelworks at Witten was bombed for the first time, eight Lancasters were shot down and half of these losses were borne by 195 Squadron at Wratting Common. In fact 195 Squadron, which had reformed at Witchford in early October, had the misfortune to suffer the heaviest losses in the *G-H* force – eleven Lancasters missing.

During December especially many heavy raids were directed against German cities and towns which so far had escaped the attention of Bomber Command. On 2nd/3rd Hagen was attacked, quickly followed by Heilbronn, Soest, Osnabruck and Ulm; although on 12/13th Essen suffered yet another heavy raid, when six Lancasters were lost out of a force of five hundred and forty (1.1%). One crew of 582 Squadron at Little Staughton was lost and amongst the crew were two airmen who had recently been awarded D.F.M.s on the completion of their tours with other squadrons.

Just two days before Christmas thirty PPF Lancasters and Mosquitos were detailed to attack the Gremberg railway yards at Cologne. The force was split into three formations, each led by an *Oboe* Lancaster. The Master Bomber was Squadron Leader Robert A.M. Palmer, D.F.C., Bar, of 109 Squadron, who was flying a Lancaster of 582 Squadron. The operation had an unfortunate start when two Lancasters of 35 Squadron collided over the French coast. On reaching the target area, where heavy cloud had been forecast, visibility was found to be clear, so a message was sent to break

Squadron Leader R.A.M. Palmer, V.C., D.F.C., Bar, of No 109 Squadron. (Imperial War Museum)

formation and bomb visually.

The signal did not reach Squadron Leader Palmer, who continued his measured and careful run onto the target despite his Lancaster having already been damaged by flak. The aircraft began to fill with smoke but he continued going, making an exact and perfect *Oboe* approach, with the bombs accurately hitting the target. His Lancaster was last seen spiralling to earth in flames and only one of the crew managed to escape. Palmer was on his third operational tour and flying his one hundred and eleventh mission. He was posthumously awarded the Victoria Cross, for 'his record of prolonged and heroic endeavour is beyond praise'. Air Vice-Marshal Bennett had predicted that should any of his airmen be awarded the V.C., it would be posthumously, such were the dangers they faced every time they flew. Another four Lancasters from 582 Squadron and one Mosquito of 109 Squadron also failed to return to Little Staughton – a disastrous night which clouded the Christmas celebrations at the airfield. However, one of the Lancaster captains, Captain E. Swales, S.A.A.F., was awarded an 'immediate' D.F.C. for his part in the raid.

Despite the heartening and dramatic reduction in the overall losses in the latter months of the year, the crews, especially the more experienced ones, were only too aware that sudden and violent death was always near at hand, a constant reminder of their precarious and tenuous hold on life. As one airman of 35 Squadron later remembered: 'It was a horrible and frightening experience to see other aircraft explode or go down in flames. More especially over the target area when you were usually on a straight run in to bomb...When you returned safely there was joy to realise that you had survived another operation but mixed with a deep sadness at what you had witnessed.'

On the penultimate night of the year (30th/31st December) when the Kalk-Nord railway yards at Cologne were attacked by a force of four hundred

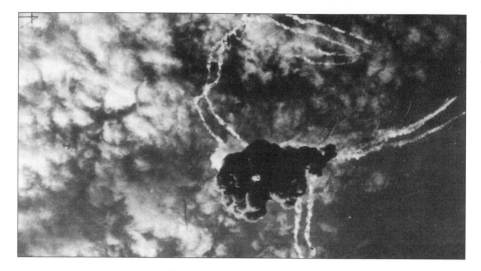

A sudden and violent death – a Lancaster explodes in flames. (via R. Matthews)

and seventy aircraft, two crews failed to return. It was considered a most successful operation, heavy damage had been inflicted on the yards and two nearby railway stations for a loss rate of 0.4%, but such figures were cold comfort to 156 Squadron at Upwood; it had lost its Commander, Wing Commander Donald B. Falconer, D.F.C., A.F.C., along with its Engineering Leader, Flight Lieutenant W.N. Bingham. Their Lancaster received a direct hit from flak and there were no survivors. Wing Commander Falconer had already completed fifty-five operations and his operational experience dated back to Hampdens; at the time of his death he had been in command of the squadron for just over five weeks. Only one of the fourteen airmen involved on the night survived as a prisoner of war.

In the briefest of periods before 1944 drew to a close, another eight aircraft were lost in action, fifty-two airmen killed and two taken prisoner. Nevertheless since mid-August the Command had flown almost 73,000 sorties and dropped over a quarter of a million tons of bombs at an overall loss rate of 1%. It was abundantly clear that the chances of surviving an operational tour were far, far greater than at any other time of the war. Nevertheless the majority of crews in Bomber Command had expected, or fondly hoped, that the war would be over before Christmas. Now they entered the Command's sixth year of war – surely victory was, at long last, not far away?

Chapter 11

Onwards and Upwards to Victory

(JANUARY-MAY 1945)

It was 'business as usual' for Bomber Command as it entered its sixth year of the air war; synthetic-oil targets, road and rail communications in western Germany and support for the Allied land forces remained its main priorities. Nevertheless Air Chief Marshal Harris continued the assault on German cities and towns almost to the end of April 1945 when the war was virtually over. Many old and familiar targets – Berlin, Essen, Düsseldorf, Hamburg, Cologne, Duisburg, Nuremberg and Stuttgart – received their last visit from the Command's crews, along with many towns that were bombed for the first time.

The Command had grown into an awesome bombing force; by March there were seventy-two heavy squadrons along with eleven Mosquito squadrons, as well as another thirteen in No 100 Group operating on bomber support duties. It was the most powerful strike force ever assembled, with the technical equipment and expertise to operate with equal facility by day and by night as well as able to bomb accurately in most weather conditions.

Overall the losses sustained by the Command during these final months of the war were relatively and remarkably light; nevertheless over five hundred and seventy aircraft were lost in action and on several operations some bitter losses were suffered, including a number of senior and experienced crews. For instance on two consecutive nights in early January, two Cambridgeshire squadrons lost a number of 'veteran' airmen. On 1st/2nd, Wing Commander R.J. Newton, D.F.C., MiD, R.N.Z.A.F., the Commander of 75 (NZ) Squadron, was killed with his seven-man crew whilst attacking railway targets at Vohwinkel. He was flying his fiftieth operation and had been in charge of the squadron for barely one month. His replacement was a twenty-two year old New Zealander, Wing Commander Cyril H. 'Mac' Baigent, D.F.C., Bar, R.N.Z.A.F., who had completed his second tour (fifty-five operations) in the previous November. Baigent was awarded a D.S.O. in October and he later commanded the squadron in New Zealand during 1947-50.

On the following night (2nd/3rd) Wing Commander K.J. Lawson,

D.S.O., Bar, D.F.C., of 405 Squadron was killed over Nuremberg; he was on his ninety-second operation. During 1945 both these squadrons sustained the heaviest losses in their respective Groups; 75 (NZ) Squadron lost eleven crews whereas 405 had ten crews missing in action. The sharp disparity of the ages of crew members at this late stage of the war can be illustrated in these missing crews – although most of the airmen were in their early twenties, two were nineteen years old and the oldest was thirty-seven.

'NE181' of No 75 (NZ) Squadron receives its one hundred and first bomb symbol at Mepal on 3rd February 1945. (via R.N.Z.A.F.)

The attack on Dresden on 13th/14th February 1945 has caused endless controversy right up to recent times. The facts

An unknown crew of No 7 Squadron at Oakington in early 1945. (via H.S. Thomas)

of the matter are that Dresden was a major road and rail centre used for supplies and troop reinforcements for the Eastern Front; therefore it was a valid transportation target. With the Russian forces fast advancing in the East, the Allied High Command decided to implement Operation *Thunderclap*, which listed Berlin, Dresden and Leipzig as likely targets, 'and associated cities where heavy attack will cause great confusion in civilian evacuation from the East and hamper movement of reinforcements from other fronts'. Thus the 'infamous' Dresden operation had been approved at the highest level. It should also be noted that the Yalta Conference, the meeting of Churchill, Roosevelt and Stalin, took place between 4th and 11th February.

The U.S.A.F. had planned a daylight operation on 13th February, which was cancelled due to 'inferior weather', with the result that over eight hundred Lancasters and Mosquitos attacked Dresden in two waves on the night of the 13th/14th when the railways yards were the specific target. Over 2,600 tons of bombs were dropped, which created a massive firestorm that left most of the city devastated. The following day the U.S.A.F. dropped over 780

Captain Edwin Swales, S.A.A.F., (fourth from the right) and his crew of No 582 Squadron in November 1944.

tons of bombs, mostly incendiaries, which only added to the conflagration. The estimates of fatalities vary between 35,000 to 125,000. In the entire subsequent furore it is hardly remarked that forty-nine R.A.F. airmen were killed and their ages ranged from nineteen to forty-two years. Nine of those airmen had flown from Cambridgeshire airfields; 405 Squadron lost one Lancaster and a Lancaster of 115 Squadron crash-landed in France.

Ten nights later (23rd/24th February) the railway yards at Pforzheim to the north-west of Stuttgart were the target for three hundred and eighty Lancaster and Mosquito crews, the first heavy raid on the town and another demonstration of the huge destructive powers of Bomber Command in these final months of the war. Captain Edwin Swales, D.F.C., S.A.A.F., of 582 Squadron at Little Staughton, was chosen to be the Master Bomber. His Lancaster was hit twice by night fighters over the target area but he continued to direct the bombing (1,825 tons in twenty-two minutes!). It was thought that about 80% of the town was destroyed with a heavy loss of civilian lives. By now Swales' Lancaster was so severely damaged that it was very difficult to control, only with considerable skill and strength did he manage to keep it sufficiently steady for his crew to bale out over Allied occupied territory. Before Swales could make his escape the aircraft hit high tension wires and plunged to the ground and he was found dead at the controls. This brave South African airman was awarded a posthumous Victoria Cross, the last of the air war. The citation read: 'Intrepid in the attack, courageous in the face of danger, he did his duty to the last, giving his life that his comrades might live…'.

During February 1945 the Commanders of three Groups (Nos 1, 4 and 5) were changed, presumably to give some senior officers the opportunity of operational control at the 'sharp end'. But perhaps what was quite remarkable, was the wealth of vastly experienced airmen in command of the stations and squadrons in Cambridgeshire. Geoff Womersley commanded Gransden Lodge, S.W.B. Menaul at Upwood, Hamish Mahaddie was in charge of Warboys, George Grant at Graveley and T. L. Bingham-Hall (an ex-Commander of 156 Squadron) was at Oakington. All had reached the rank of Group Captain and all had a vast and deep knowledge of operational flying.

The same applied to the Squadron Commanders. Wing Commanders Somerville and Baigent have already been noted. In April another 'youngster', Wing Commander A. J. L. Craig, D.S.O., D.F.C., took over command of 156 Squadron; like Baigent he was only twenty-two years old and had previously served in 7 and 35 Squadrons. In 1946 he led 35 Squadron on a goodwill tour of the United States. But perhaps the one Squadron Commander who may be said to epitomise the wartime Command was Wing Commander J.R.G. 'Roy' Ralston, D.S.O., Bar, A.F.C., D.F.M.; in March he was given

Wing Commander J.R.G. 'Roy' Ralston, D.S.O., Bar, A.F.C., D.F.M., became the Commander of No 139 Squadron at Upwood in March 1945. (R.A.F. Museum)

the command of 139 Squadron at Upwood. Roy Ralston was yet another 'Halton brat', who had steadily worked his way up from a Sergeant pilot in Blenheims (a 'Blenheim boy') before flying Mosquitos with 105 Squadron. Ralston had completed eighty-two operations and the award of a Bar to his D.S.O. read 'his unswerving devotion to duty and heroic endeavours have set a standard beyond praise'. These brave airmen and countless others like them had managed to survive against unimaginable odds and dangers but yet their names have been largely forgotten, except, of course, by the rapidly dwindling Bomber Command survivors.

It was in March 1945 that Bomber Command reached its pinnacle and fully demonstrated its overwhelming strength and power; over 21,000 sorties were flown by day and night for the loss of two hundred and seventy aircraft (1.27%). On four separate occasions over 1,000 crews were in action – on one night (7th/8th) 1,276 crews were in action, the highest number ever, and this massive operation was followed by three heavy raids on successive days (11th to 13th) when a total of 10,600 tons of bombs were dropped on

Hamburg in 1945: one of the heavily damaged German cities. (via R. Matthews)

three targets in the Ruhr – Essen, Dortmund and Wuppertal. On 1st March, Goebbels, the German Propaganda Minister, recorded in his diary: 'The air war has now turned into a crazy orgy. We are totally defenceless against it. The Reich will be gradually turned into a complete desert.' A fortnight later he wrote: 'The morale of the German people, both at home and at the front, is sinking even lower…the people are thoroughly despondent.'

On 7th/8th March three separate towns – Dessau, Hemmingstedt and Harburg – were targeted and the Command lost forty-one aircraft (3.2%) out of the 1,276 in action that night, its heaviest loss in 1945. The PFF and 35 Squadron, in particular, lost a most experienced and highly respected leader, Squadron Leader D.B. Elliott, D.F.C., 2 Bars. He was acting as Master Bomber over an oil refinery at Hemmingstadt; Elliott and his seven crewmen were killed. He had flown his first operation back in April 1943 and was then on his eighty-ninth operation.

On this night a most disturbing fact emerged. Six airmen of a Lancaster crew of 195 Squadron managed to parachute safely whilst attacking Dessau to the south-west of Berlin. They and their aircraft came down at Battelstadt about eighty miles west of Dresden. They were captured and handed over to the members of the S.S., who shot them. Up until then the squadron had experienced a run of good luck, in fact this was the only Lancaster it lost in 1945. On the same night another airman, the only survivor of a Lancaster crew of 103 Squadron, suffered the same fate at the hands of the local police. He had landed safely in the same area. During March another twenty-three airmen are *known* to have been murdered in a similar manner. It is a matter of conjecture whether the Dresden raid had brought about this brutal treatment of captured airmen; certainly the German people's hostility and aggression to bomber crews had become more marked. Although it should be noted that during this period two hundred and twenty-five airmen parachuted and landed safely and were taken into captivity; so it would appear that it was a matter of luck to which authority they were handed over when captured. Of course, the crews flying at this time were unaware of this additional hazard; these war crimes were only uncovered after the war.

Although the *Luftwaffe* was critically starved of aviation fuel, it was not quite 'on its knees'; its night-fighter force still posed problems for the crews. On 16th/17th March that *bête noir* of Bomber Command – Nuremberg – brought about the loss of twenty-four aircraft when it was bombed for the last time; most were shot down by night fighters. It was almost one year since that horrendous Nuremberg mission. Seven aircraft were known to have been shot down by the *Luftwaffe*'s turbo-jet fighters, Messerschmitt Me 262As, on 31st March when the Blohm & Voss shipyards in Hamburg were bombed, where it was thought they were assembling the new and more powerful 'Snorkel' U-boats. On this operation eleven aircraft (2.3%) failed to return, the last occasion the Command's losses exceeded nine. Seven nights

later the crews returned to Hamburg and another eight crews were lost. This proved to be the last major raid on Hamburg, one of the most heavily damaged German cities, which had been first bombed in May 1940.

Without doubt the shining stars of Bomber Command during 1945 were the Mosquito squadrons of the Light Night Striking Force, which by the end of January totalled eight; 163 Squadron had reformed at Wyton under the command of Wing Commander Ivor Broom, D.F.C., A.F.C., who later became an Air Marshal. The crews of this relatively small force roamed the skies with impunity, only the Me 262As posed any threat to them – although only one Mosquito is known to have fallen to a Me 262A. On 27th/28th March a crew of 139 Squadron returning from Berlin was shot down; the pilot, Flight Lieutenant A.A.J. Amsterdam, D.F.C., who was a Dutchman and a highly experienced airman, was flying his one hundred and first operational sortie. He was just one of many such airmen serving in the LNSF and unfortunately quite a number of them failed to survive the war.

The year opened in impressive style for the 'Mossie' crews when, on 1st January, seventeen attacked fourteen railway tunnels in the Eifel region between the Rhine and the Ardennes. The crews were required to place their time-fused 4,000 lb bombs into the entrances of the tunnels from a height of about 200 ft, and only one crew (from 692 Squadron) was brought down by light flak. After attacking Kochem tunnel Flight Lieutenant H.H. Tattersall of 571 Squadron at Oakington was awarded an 'immediate' D.F.C. for his actions on this operation.

The 'Mossie' crews were frequently in action in weather conditions which

Mosquitos of No 128 Squadron at Wyton about to leave on the 'Berlin Express'.
(via C.M. Harris)

grounded the Main Force. Countless German cities and towns suffered 'nuisance' raids or 'siren tours', as they were known but they also attacked oil targets. The Light Night Striking Force's lasting claim to fame during the final months of the war was that from 20th/21st February until 20th/ 21st April its crews bombed Berlin on fifty-three nights and during one period they attacked 'The Big City' on thirty-six consecutive nights. These operations became known as 'The Berlin Express' or 'Milk Train'; there were three different routes there and back, which were named Platforms One, Two and Three! Many of these operations became almost routine – one pilot's log book read: 'Big raid, over 100 aircraft. Did Dly Telegraph X-word on the way back.'

On 20th/21st April the last bombs were dropped on Berlin by a Mosquito crew of 109 Squadron; almost five years after the first bombs fell on the German capital on 25/26th August 1940. During 1945 fifty Mosquitos were lost in action and seventy-five airmen killed but amongst this number were at least six airmen who had completed over sixty operations. As the Command Headquarters stated: 'The value of the Mosquito attacks as a supplement to the attacks by heavy aircraft is unquestioned and their contribution to the success of the combined bomber offensive was both significant and praiseworthy.'

It is probably right and proper to consider the Avro Lancaster as

179

Two Lancasters on their way to the island of Wangerooge on 25th April 1945.

another 'hero' of Bomber Command; it was arguably the finest and most successful Allied heavy bomber. It was much loved by Air Chief Marshal Harris and held in great affection by its crews. A total of 150,000 Lancaster sorties were flown, almost double that of any other heavy bomber and four hundred and thirty-one were lost in action (2.2%). Sixty-two squadrons were equipped with Lancasters and, in 1945, nine were operating from Cambridgeshire airfields, so low-flying Lancasters were a familiar sight in the skies.

Only thirty-five individual Lancasters managed to achieve over one hundred sorties and quite remarkably four of them were operating from airfields in Cambridgeshire – ND709 *Flying Kiwi* with 405 Squadron, ND875 *Nuts* of 156 Squadron, ME803 *L for Love* at Witchford with 115 Squadron and NE181 *Mike the Captain's Fancy* of 75 (NZ) Squadron at Mepal. More than any other aircraft, the Lancaster epitomised Bomber Command during the last three years of the war.

It might be said that a greater hazard for crews during these last few months was the risk of mid-air collision with 'friendly' aircraft. It has been reckoned that no less than forty-five aircraft were lost in this unfortunate manner during 1945, which resulted in the deaths of over two hundred and fifty airmen. The most tragic operation in this respect was on 25th April when over four hundred and eighty were despatched to bomb the coastal batteries on the island of Wangerooge, which controlled the sea approaches to the ports of Bremen and Wilhelmshaven. Seven aircraft were lost, six as a result of mid-air collisions; forty-one airmen killed within the last two weeks of the war. It may be recalled that back in mid-December 1939, Bomber Command had suffered its first heavy losses in the same area.

Earlier on the same day over three hundred and seventy Lancasters and Mosquitos, strongly escorted by R.A.F. and U.S.A.A.F. long-range fighters, were sent to Berchtesgaden in the Bavarian Alps to bomb Hitler's 'Eagle's Nest' and the nearby S.S. guard barracks; there was a concern that fanatical Nazis might use the area for a final and desperate last stand. The barracks were flattened but Hitler's villa escaped unscathed because the height of the mountains obscured the *Oboe* signals and the heavy mist prevented visual bombing. Not a single *Luftwaffe* fighter took to the air to oppose the force but two Lancasters were lost (probably to flak), seven airmen killed and another seven taken prisoner.

The following day (26th April) most Lancaster squadrons were involved in Operation *Exodus*, the early evacuation of freed prisoners of war from airfields in Belgium. Each Lancaster could carry twenty-four passengers and until 7th May a total of some 72,000 POWs were brought home safely, a remarkable total in such a short period of time. Sadly these flights did not

A Lancaster being loaded with food supplies during Operation Manna.

proceed without a few accidents; the most tragic occurred on 9th May when a Lancaster of 415 Squadron from Waterbeach crashed whilst trying to land at Juvincourt in northern France after experiencing control problems. Everybody on board was killed, the six-man crew and twenty-four ex-prisoners, all Army personnel.

Another pleasurable and satisfying operation for the crews during the same period, was the supply of food to the starving people in western Holland, which was still in enemy hands; these operations were known as *Manna*. The local German Commander had agreed to a truce to allow food supplies to be dropped at certain nominated airfields and the racecourse at The Hague. Crews of 115 Squadron made the first *Manna* drops; in fact back in the first week of April its crews had given a demonstration of low-flying at Witchford to a gathering of Air Ministry officials and the Command's 'top brass'. From 29th April until 7th May over 2,830 Lancaster crews, along with one hundred and twenty-four Mosquito crews to mark the 'targets', were engaged in dropping some 6,600 tons of food supplies.

Considering the immense contribution made by the Mosquitos during the last stages of the war, it was perhaps fitting that on 2nd/3rd May 1945 almost one hundred and eighty 'Mossie' crews were engaged in Bomber Command's final operation, bombing the port of Kiel and also airfields in the area. Again most appropriately, twelve crews of 139 Squadron at Upwood were in action on this last day of the air war as just one squadron crew had flown the very first Bomber Command sortie from Wyton on 3rd September 1939; all twelve crews returned safely. However, the supporting crews of No 100 Group were not so lucky, three were lost: a Mosquito of 169 Squadron, which was shot down whilst attacking an airfield and two Halifaxes of 199 Squadron were believed to have collided. Fifteen airmen were killed, the last brave airmen to lose their lives in action whilst serving in Bomber Command.

Bomber Command's long and bitter war had finally ended and no other Allied force had waged such a prolonged and continuous battle. Its crews had been in action for 71% of the total nights of the war and slightly over half of the days. The Command had lost 8,953 aircraft, 55,500 airmen killed, and another 8,400 wounded with 9,830 taken prisoner. It had been a monumental effort by the 125,000 airmen that had served in Bomber Command in the Second World War. They all deserve the country's praise and honour.

Chapter 12

Farewell
'Bomber Men'
A Job Well Done

O n VE Day, 8th May 1945, ceremonial parades and parties were held at the various bomber stations throughout Cambridgeshire. A day of celebration, but also a time to remember those friends and colleagues who had perished in the conflict; at last there was the opportunity to look forward to returning home to a 'normal' life.

A line had been drawn under each squadron's wartime record and its contribution to the Command's long and bitter campaign. At Witchford, 115 Squadron had completed almost six years of continuous service with the Command, its crews had flown the second highest number of sorties and it was the only squadron to have lost over two hundred aircraft in action (two hundred and eight). The squadron was closely followed by 75 (NZ) at Mepal with one hundred and thirty-three aircraft lost whilst flying the highest number of sorties – over 8,000 in a total of seven hundred and ninety-three operations. Whereas in the PFF, 7 Squadron at Oakington had the dubious honour of losing the most number of PFF aircraft – one hundred and sixty-five. Without doubt all the airmen and airwomen of the eighteen bomber squadrons in Cambridgeshire could take immense pride in their war record; before the end of the year seven of these squadrons would be disbanded.

Air Vice-Marshal Bennett was quick in sending his personal thanks to all those serving in his Group. On 8th May his message arrived at the eight PFF stations:

> Bomber Command's share in this great effort has been a major one. You, each one of you, have made that possible. The Pathfinder Force has shouldered a grave responsibility. It has led Bomber Command, the greatest striking force ever known. That we have been successful can be seen in the far reaching effects, which the bomber offensive has achieved. That is the greatest record the Pathfinder Force ever hopes to achieve; for those results have benefited all law abiding people…I want to thank you, each man and woman of you, personally and to congratulate you on your unrelenting spirit and energy and on the results you have achieved …Happiness to you all – always Keep Pressing On Along the Path of Peace.

Just four days later Bennett, the only wartime Group Commander not to be knighted, was succeeded by Air Vice-Marshal J.R. Whitley. By the end of the year the PFF was disbanded as there was no future envisaged for it in the post-war Bomber Command. Over sixty years later the exploits of the Pathfinder airmen (3,727 were killed) are still held in awe. They were, and remain, an 'elite' band of airmen. Their memory is perpetuated in the fine Pathfinders Museum at R.A.F. Wyton, which opened in 1996.

On 10th May Air Chief Marshal Harris issued a Special Order of the Day, it conveyed his appreciation to all those serving in his Command:

> To you who survived, I would say this. Content yourself, and take credit with those that perished and now that the 'Cease Fire' has sounded countless homes within our Empire will welcome back a father, husband or son whose life, but for your endeavours and your sacrifices, would assuredly have been expended during long further years of agony to achieve a victory already ours. No Allied Nation is clear of this debt to you.

Those survivors of Bomber Command did not realise that this would be almost the last acknowledgement and praise for their vital contribution to the Allied victory for many decades to come. Although really none sought such accolades, as they considered that they were only 'doing their duty'. Quite remarkably, Winston Churchill's VE Address to the Nation on 13th May did not contain any reference to, let alone praise for, the six year bombing campaign; it was almost as if the strategic bombing offensive had never taken place. Air Chief Marshal Harris's subsequent endeavours to obtain a Campaign Medal for all his airmen and airwomen went unheeded, as indeed have several other attempts over the years, which even at this distance of time seems to be a national disgrace.

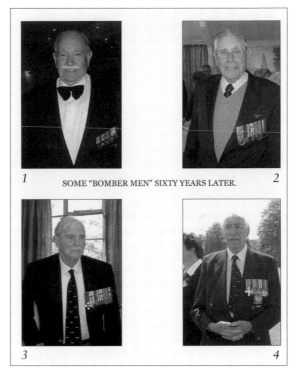

SOME "BOMBER MEN" SIXTY YEARS LATER.

1. *(Warrant Officer) J.C. 'Charlie' Chapman, D.F.M.;*
2. *(Warrant Officer) J. 'Jack' Watson, D.F.M.;*
3. *(Group Captain) G. 'Geoff' Womersley, D.S.O., Bar, D.F.C., MiD;*
4. *(Flight Lieutenant) H. 'Harold' Hernaman, D.F.C.*

In the post-war decades, of all the Allied Commanders-in-Chief Sir Arthur Harris became almost a *persona non grata*, except of course to his airmen who would hear no ill spoken of 'Old Butch'. It became the fashion to criticise and condemn Harris and his prosecution of the bombing offensive both on strategic and moral grounds, despite the fact that the *Official History* (published in 1961) deemed that 'the enduring courage, determination and conviction of Sir Arthur Harris, who bore the responsibility for more than three years, deserves to be commemorated.'

Even now many surviving aircrew still feel betrayed by such criticism, especially when they remember so many friends and colleagues that were killed. Such historic judgements, however correct or incorrect, should not in any way detract from recognition of the immense bravery of all the aircrews who served in Bomber Command throughout its long, bitter and costly war. As their revered leader 'Butch' Harris said at a Bomber Command Reunion in 1977, 'You have never been given adequate recognition for your decisive part in the defeat of Hitler. You inflicted on the Germans the greatest of all their lost battles. But in all the war histories this is underestimated and you have been subjected to the sneers and smears of so-called historians.'

The splendid Runnymede Memorial at Cooper's Hill, Surrey. 'Their name liveth for evermore.'

As in life, so in death, Harris remained a figure of some controversy: he died in April 1984, aged 91. When it was announced in 1991 that a statue of him was to be erected in the precinct of the R.A.F.'s church, St Clement Danes in central London, some members of the national media took the opportunity to reopen all the arguments against Harris and the strategic bombing offensive, although the statue was not publicly financed. It was finally unveiled by H.M. Queen Elizabeth The Queen Mother on 31st May 1992, and it stands appropriately close to that of Lord Dowding, the Battle of Britain Commander-in-Chief.

Considering such responses in the media and in print it is perhaps not surprising that those survivors of Bomber Command formed flourishing associations where they could renew the strong and deep bonds of friendship that had been made during the long and dark days and nights of the war. The Pathfinders Association was formed in 1945 and the Aircrew Association in 1977. There were, and still are, countless Squadron Associations and in 1985 the Bomber Command Association was formed; one of its aims was 'as a means of continuing the comradeship that had been forged in the heat of battle and perpetuating the Command's history with truth dignity and pride'.

Over the last fifteen years or so there have been a number of published works to finally 'put the record straight' that Bomber Command played a vital role in the Allied victory over Germany and that its airmen and airwomen made a larger contribution to victory in Europe than any comparable force. The year 2002 was designated a Commemorative Year for Bomber Command, sixty years since the arrival of Sir

Memorial stones at: 1) Wratting Common;
2) Upwood; 3) Little Staughton;
4) Graveley; 5) Warboys.

Arthur Harris as Commander-in-Chief and the first '1,000 bomber raid'. In 2006 the Imperial War Museum North at Salford mounted an exhibition titled *Against The Odds*, which told 'the extraordinary and controversial story of Bomber Command in the Second World War'. It claimed to be the first major exhibition devoted to Bomber Command. Sixty-one years is a rather long time to take to publicly recognise and celebrate Bomber Command's 'extraordinary story' – but perhaps better late than never!

Many of the airmen who lost their lives whilst serving in Bomber Command are buried in the several War Cemeteries in Germany. But those who have no known graves are commemorated at the splendid Commonwealth Air Forces' Runnymede Memorial at Cooper's Hill, Surrey. Over 20,450 names are listed and a high percentage of them are Bomber Command airmen.

Cambridgeshire has a fair number of memorials to the airmen that flew from its bomber airfields. There are fine stained glass windows in Ely Cathedral, St Bartholomew's church, Great Gransden, St Mary Magdalene's church, Warboys and at R.A.F. Wyton. Memorial stones can be found at Graveley, Little Staughton, Mepal, Wratting Common, Witchford, Upwood and Warboys, and the Oakington village sign commemorates

The Lancaster (PA474) of the Battle of Britain Memorial Flight honouring the 'Bomber Men' at Warboys in May 2006.

No 7 Squadron. There is also a small exhibition devoted to the airfields at Mepal and Witchford at the Lancaster Business Park, Witchford, which is on the site of the latter airfield.

Although the Pathfinder Association was disbanded in 2002, its Annual Reunion Service is still held in St Mary Magdalene's church, Warboys, on a Sunday in early May. It has become the custom for the villagers to provide a buffet lunch in the village hall for the veterans, their relatives and friends. In recent years these moving reunions have been further enhanced by a fly-past of the Lancaster of the Battle of Britain Memorial Flight, flown by Flight Lieutenant Edwin 'Ed' Straw. The Lancaster, PA474, has recently undergone a major service and for the 2007 season will carry the name *The Phantom of the Ruhr* and the markings 'HW-R' and 'BQ-B', of 100 and 550 Squadrons respectively.

The author with a 21st Century Lancaster pilot – Flight Lieutenant Edwin 'Ed' Straw of the Battle of Britain Memorial Flight.

The unmistakable sound of its Merlin engines and the unforgettable sight of the Lancaster passing low over the playing grounds to the rear of the hall bring tears of emotion to the veterans; their Lancaster memories are theirs alone. To be present on such an occasion, in their company, is indeed a rare honour. The courage, determination and resolve of the 'Bomber Men' must never ever be forgotten.

Bibliography

Ashworth, Chris, *R.A.F. Bomber Command, 1936-1968*, Patrick Stephens, 1993

Barker, Ralph, *The Thousand Plan: The Story of the First Thousand Bomber Raid on Cologne*, Chatto & Windus, 1965

Bowyer, Chaz, *Bomber Barons*, William Kimber, 1983

Bowyer, Michael, *2 Group: A Complete History 1936-1945*, Faber & Faber, 1974

Chorley, W.R., *R.A.F. Bomber Command Losses in the Second World War*, Vols 1-5, Midland Publications, 1992-1998

Cooper, Alan W., *Bombers Over Berlin: the R.A.F. Offensive November 1943-March 1944*, William Kimber, 1985

Delve, Ken, *Bomber Command, 1936-1968: An Operational and Historical Record*, Pen & Sword, 2005

Delve, Ken, & Jacobs, P., *The Six Year Offensive*, Arms & Armour, 1992

Falconer, Jonathan, *Bomber Command Handbook*, Sutton Publishing, 1998

Ford-Jones, M., *Bomber Squadron: The Men Who Flew With XV*, William Kimber, 1987

Franks, Norman, *Forever Strong: The Story of No 75 RNZAF*, Random House, 1991

Goulding, A.G., *Uncommon Valour*, Air Data Publications, 1996

Gunby, D., *Sweeping the Skies*, Pentland Press, 1995

Harris, Sir Arthur, *Bomber Offensive*, Collins, 1947

Hastings, Max, *Bomber Command*, Michael Joseph, 1979

Jackson, R., *Before the Storm: The Story of Bomber Command, 1939-42*, Arthur Barker, 1972

Longmate, Norman, *The Bombers: The R.A.F. Offensive Against Germany, 1939-1945*, Hutchinson, 1983

Middlebrook, Martin, *The Bomber Command Diaries*, Viking, 1985

Musgrove, Gordon, *Pathfinder Force: The Story of 8 (PFF) Group*, Macdonald & Jane's, 1976

Overy, Richard, *Bomber Command, 1939-45: Reaping the Whirlwind*, Harper/Collins, 1996

Revie, Alastair, *The Lost Command*, David Bruce & Watson, 1971

Richards, Denis, *The Hardest Victory: R.A.F. Bomber Command in the Second World War*, Hodder & Stoughton, 1994

Searby, John H., *The Great Raid: Peenemunde – 17th August 1943*, Nutshell Press, 1978

Wadsworth, Michael, *They Led the Way: The Story of Pathfinder Squadron 156*, Highgate Publications (Beverley) Ltd., 1992

Index